THE SPARK THAT CHANGED EVERYTHING

Veena Prasad's writing spans diverse genres and age groups, but what she enjoys best is combining science and history in fun ways for young readers. She also teaches English literature and creates crosswords for her weekly column in *The Hindu Young World*.

Veena believes there is hope yet for the planet, if we all make sustainable life choices. On her part, she strives to minimize the trash she generates by refusing single-use disposables, and composting her organic waste, so her young readers are not burdened with the task of cleaning up the planet!

THE SPARK THAT CHANGED EVERYTHING

Stories of the World's Greatest
Discoveries, Ideas and Inventions

VEENA PRASAD

hachette
INDIA

First published in 2019 by Hachette India
(Registered name: Hachette Book Publishing India Pvt. Ltd)
An Hachette UK company
www.hachetteindia.com

SRD

ISBN 978-93-88322-64-5

Hachette Book Publishing India Pvt. Ltd
4th & 5th Floors, Corporate Centre
Plot No. 94, Sector 44, Gurugram – 122003, India

Typeset in Chaparral Pro by Manmohan Kumar, Delhi

Printed and bound in India
by Manipal Technologies Limited, Manipal

MIX
Paper | Supporting responsible forestry
FSC™ C043100
FSC
www.fsc.org

To my parents, Satyalakshmi and Rama Prasad

My mother, whose expert dissection of a hibiscus flower, forever etched in my mind, instilled in me a curiosity for the unknown, and my father, who, by generously letting me play with his box of tools (filled with sharp and dangerous things ☺), eliminated from me a fear of the unknown.

Contents

Introduction

Ideas have a way of appearing out of nowhere, and then, after a while, settling quietly down in our lives while we give no more thought to them. Like say, eating a fully cooked meal, prepared with grains, pulses, vegetables on the side (as a salad, if you like, or a cooked preparation with cuisine-specific masalas), and maybe you're eating this meal off a steel plate or a porcelain one, maybe you're using a spoon and fork to do so... Maybe you want an ice cream after this meal. So you grab a jacket, head down to the ice-cream parlour, pick your flavour and pay for it.

Or you might want to call some friends over to play something. Maybe you like football or cricket, or board games, or maybe you like to chill with a book. Like this one you're holding.

A lot of ideas have gone into making this possible, and I'm not just talking about the contents. I'm talking about the papers that were bound to make this book, the idea of binding papers together, the ink that was used to print these words, the idea of putting thoughts down in words, the idea of words... And about the store you got this book from, the idea of selling something, and receiving money in exchange... About the building you're in right now, perhaps a bookstore, perhaps your home, the idea of a home, of the materials used to construct, of the principles of construction, architecture and design...

This book is about the *very first ideas*. Before there were houses, there was the idea that families could stay together as a unit, the idea of community, of villages or cities, of kingdoms or countries, of civilizations. Before there were stores and businesses, there was the idea that one could sell and buy, and use some form of money to do so. Before there were cars, someone had to invent the wheel, and before that, there was the *need* to do so.

Before there was ice cream, there was the discovery of dairy farming, of milk, and the domestication of cows. And before rice, came the idea of cultivation, agriculture, of harvesting a grain that could be cooked and eaten, and before that, the idea of cooking and preparing a meal. But before all of that, before any big human idea could be born, there was fire.

Fire – that powerful element that is as deadly as it is useful. If humans had not discovered fire and understood how to control it and stop and start it at will, there would be no cooking, no baking, no pottery, no weapons, no manufacturing, no industry... nothing that one might classify as a human 'thing'.

In this book, we trace the origins of human ingenuity, and you could say pretty much all of it started with fire.

1

Fire, Fire, Burning Bright

One million years ago, in a dark and damp cave somewhere on prehistoric earth

A group of hominins huddled together, taking shelter from the rain. They were not exactly humans – not Homo sapiens like you and me – but a slightly different species from whom we evolved.

The rain was particularly fierce that night. The group huddled closer and wondered if the sky was going to be split by the big flash of light. Soon enough it was. A second later, there was a booming sound that thudded in their hearts.

The rain stopped, but the light continued to fork across the sky. The hominins stared as the light from the sky reached the ground. It seemed as if the *sun* had come down to earth! A yellow blaze enveloped a tree and began to crackle and spread, swallowing up everything it touched. The hominins hopped and danced with a mixture of fear and excitement. They hooted and grunted and howled at this strange phenomenon. They were not using words (language hadn't been invented yet) but communicated with sounds and gestures.

One young hominin, more curious than the rest, broke away from the group and began to run towards the blazing light. Those who saw her made warning noises, but she was too far to hear, or care.

Who/What Are Hominins?

Hominins are the ancestors of humans. Around seven million years ago, two evolutionary lines branched out from a common ancestor: the line of the great apes and the line of humans. Great apes evolved into gorillas, bonobos and chimpanzees. All the species that make up the human line are grouped as hominins. They include early human-like beings who walked on two legs and probably used tools. Some of the hominin species are Australopithecus afarensis, Homo habilis, Homo neanderthalensis, Homo erectus and Homo sapiens. The last one refers to us – modern humans – the only surviving species of hominins.

She kept running towards the glow, ignoring the rocks and spiky vegetation underfoot. She was used to all that, having explored the area many times before. But this yellow light was strange and new, and she would not stop until her curiosity was satisfied.

Meanwhile, in the cave, the rest of the hominins prepared to sleep. It was a freezing night, so they lay close to each other, hoping that the collective warmth of their bodies would be enough to keep them all alive till sunrise. As for the one who had run away, she would probably never return.

It really was cold that night. They wrapped their arms around each other, but the biting cold chilled them to the bone.

But then they heard something that sent a different sort of chill down their spine. It was a shuffling sound coming from outside the cave. Could it be a wild animal? They sprang up and shrank back against the walls of the cave, grabbing the sticks and stones that lay around.

With bated breath, they waited to see what sort of animal would enter.

A strange creature that shone like a small sun appeared before them. What could it be?

It did not attack them or make a sound, so they all moved in to take a closer look.

It was the girl who had run away! And in her hand was a branch that was glowing red at one end.

She placed the branch slowly on the ground. The hominins were confused by it, but there was a warmth around it that was most welcome that night. It was not blazing or growing, so it must be safe.

They sat around the branch and stared at it, mesmerized.

One of them tried to touch the glowing red thing, but withdrew his hand quickly when he felt pain. It was not like the pain from a scratch or an animal bite or a bee sting – it was new, a pain he didn't understand.

The glow then started to fade. The hominins did not know what to do. They could not pick it up; it would hurt them. They sighed. And the air that escaped their mouths brightened the glow! What did this mean? Would air from their mouths keep this thing alive? Carefully, they blew again. The glow became brighter! But in their enthusiasm, they blew too hard, and the glow dimmed again. Oh no! They *had* to keep it alive. By trial and error, they figured out the perfect speed and intensity with which to blow. At one point, a little blaze erupted from the embers. It seemed to grow tongues, dancing and licking, giving off so much heat that the hominins had to move away from it. They were now scared. Was it really a good thing? Or would it kill them all? It had certainly helped them survive the cold night.

A few adventurous hominins, including the little girl who had boldly carried the glowing branch back to them all, ventured out of the cave, towards the charred part of the forest. They explored the area, careful to avoid burns from the still-hot embers but eager to understand what fire did to other things. A charred rabbit carcass, for instance, smelled good and was carried back into the cave. The meat was easy to chew, and the taste wasn't bad either, with half-cooked berries and fruits on the side!

As you probably know, a stomach full of tasty food has this way of leading us to some pretty good ideas. Read on to discover more about the earliest sparks that forged our identity as humankind.

How Does a Fire Start?

Three ingredients have to come together to start a fire: oxygen, fuel and a spark. Once the fire gets going, it will last as long as there is enough heat, oxygen and fuel. When one or more of these ingredients is no longer available, the fire dies.

Natural fires are usually started by lightning. Storm clouds contain particles of rain, ice or snow that are constantly colliding with each other, building up static electricity. Ions start jumping all over the place, charging the air negatively. This results in an 'imbalance', and so the electrons need to flow until they find positively charged particles to restore balance. The earth and objects like building spires and trees become positively charged. The electrons flow down in a streak of electricity – this is lightning.

Lightning is extremely hot. In a flash, it can reach temperatures five times hotter than the surface of the sun. When this strikes the earth, the vegetation acts as a fuel source and catches fire. Even if it had been raining earlier, the extreme heat simply vaporizes the water.

How, when and why humans thought of replicating this is a mystery. It is one thing to carry a burning ember back to a cave and keep it going, but how did anyone create a fire from scratch?

It took more than a scratch, actually. It took several strikes. It so happens that stones of the flint or pyrite variety when struck together emit sparks. Flint is a type of quartz, an extremely hard rock (almost as hard as diamond), and pyrite contains iron and sulphur. When struck together, tiny flecks of pyrite fly into the air. Because of their chemical composition, these flecks ignite spontaneously on contact with oxygen. And we have a spark! If these sparks fall on something flammable, such as dry leaves or bark, you get a fire.

Fire of Ages

Exactly how long ago humans learnt this trick is still under investigation. From archaeological findings, we know for sure that it was definitely not later than 2,30,000 years ago, and it could well be as early as 1.5 million years ago.

What is clear, however, is that the discovery of fire sparked a plethora of ideas that defined humankind.

One of the earliest ideas had to do with the very stone that was used to start a fire: Stone Age tools made from flint show signs of being treated with fire. Why? When a stone is heated to high temperatures, it flakes well, making it easier to fashion into a sharp-edged blade. Archaeologists have found different types of heat-treated hunting tools such as spear tips, arrow heads, blades of hand axes and projectiles. These tools completely changed the course of human history, marking the beginning of the idea that humans could control their environment.

How Do We Know All This?

What you just read is a story pieced together with science, history and a bit of imagination. Ancient sites of human habitation in different parts of the world have remains of bones, charred earth, tools and other things that our ancestors left behind. Scientists study these remains to understand human history.

But how do they know how old these remains are?

One of the most reliable methods of figuring out the age of ancient things is radioactive dating.

Radioactivity is the process by which certain elements (like uranium, potassium and rhenium) emit radiation and transform into other elements (like lead, argon and osmium respectively).

Now here's the interesting bit – every radioactive element has a property known as 'half-life', which is the number of years for half of the original element to turn into a new element.

For example, uranium-238 has a half-life of 4.47 billion years. This means that if you have a sample of uranium-238 with you, in 4.47 billion years, half of the atoms in the sample will turn into lead-206. And in the next 4.7 billion years, half of the remaining atoms of uranium-238 will turn into lead-206. And in the next 4.7 billion years, half of the remaining uranium-238 will... you get the idea.

So how is this useful for determining the age of things?

You can measure the number of atoms of the original radioactive material (say uranium-238) and the number of atoms of the transformed material (lead-206), and then, with a bit of clever maths, you can calculate the time it would have taken for this transformation to happen.

At the simplest instance, half of your sample could consist of uranium-238 and the other half of lead-206, which means that the sample you hold is 4.47 billion years old.

If a quarter of all atoms are uranium-238 and the rest are lead-206, you know that two half-lives have passed, so the sample must be 8.94 billion years old.

If the amount of uranium-238 is a little more than quarter but less than half, you can confidently say that the age of the sample is between 4.47 and 8.94 billion years old.

2

From Wanderers to Settlers

Humans were nomads for the longest time. They would form small groups of 10 or 12 adults and their children. These groups moved from place to place, hunting wild animals and gathering fruits and berries. Their diet consisted of meat, fruits, nuts, roots and, perhaps, insects. They stayed in one place as long as it offered enough to eat, and as long as there were no predators around. If the place proved too difficult to survive in, they would just move on.

We call them hunter-gatherers.

They lived in caves or other temporary shelters. Archaeologists have found a cave in the Gesher Benot Ya'aqov province of Israel containing evidence of human habitation that is almost 8,00,000 years old. There are remains of more than 55 different kinds of edible vegetation. This means that these hunter-gatherers had studied plant life extensively and knew what was edible and what was not.

At some point, they came to understand how plants grow. They figured out that a seed sprouts under the right conditions and, when put into soil and watered, grows into a plant. They began doing this over large patches of ground. This was the first instance of agriculture. All this happened sometime between 23,000 and 12,000 years ago.

At around the same time, they started building more permanent residences, because if your food grows on a patch of land near your dwelling, it makes sense to stay there. They also learnt to domesticate animals. Smaller and more submissive animals were easy to domesticate, and they were used for protection, hunting, labour and food.

And then there was fire. We always come back to fire.

Fire made it possible to cook food. Along with making meat and roots easier to chew, it also made accessible a whole new set of plants that humans were unable to eat before the idea of cooking emerged. Take potatoes, for instance. You can't eat them raw. But once cooked (or fried), you can't stop eating them! The same goes for grains and legumes. Our non-cooking ancestors would think us daft for including those hard, stone-like pulses in an essential diet. But cooking makes them softer and easier to digest. Today, we take it for granted that preparing a meal involves cooking. However, our ancestors would have followed a recipe of this sort:

A Non-Cooking Ancestor's Recipe

Cook time: Zero minutes.

Prep time: Anywhere between 30 minutes and several days, depending on how good a hunter you are.

Ingredients: Lean meat, fish, insects, larvae, seeds, berries, fruits, nuts, roots, eggs, honey.

Method: Pick it up, clean (optional) and eat it.

Our non-cooking ancestors would also be surprised by our love for milk and other dairy products, as they were most likely lactose intolerant. They would probably nod approvingly at our choice of fruit, but their larger sizes (compared to the wild varieties) would astonish them. Even now, if you happen to stumble upon wild apples or strawberries, you will find them to be much smaller in size than the ones in a market. And they taste different, too.

The idea of growing and cooking our food made a BIG difference in the course of human evolution.

For one thing, humans stopped being nomads. Since food was rooted in local land, they no longer had to forage deep inside forests. They started settling in places with fertile soil and access to water. This was the first step towards creating what we know as a society.

How Cultivation Led to Civilization

Step 1: Grow food.

Step 2: Stay put.

Step 3: Build houses.

Step 4: Make friends with neighbours.

Step 5: Become farmers and hunters.

Step 6: Call yourselves a tribe.

Step 7: Make rules for peaceful coexistence.

Step 8: Grow so much food that you can feed others.

Step 9: Have everyone do different things – make tools for the farmer, make weapons for the hunter.

Step 10: Grow prosperous, safeguard your property and defend your village.

Step 11: Become soldiers and leaders who decide the best way to protect the village.

Step 12: Become artists, artisans and traders in times of prosperity.

And this is how villages grow into towns, into cities, into countries... A culture evolves, and civilizations are formed. There are tribes and clansmen; villages and chieftains; kingdoms and kings; empires and emperors; countries and democratically elected leaders.

How Does Fire Change Food?

Cooking food causes both chemical and biological changes. The chemical changes make food easier to chew, so the process of eating is faster. To understand how much faster, compare the 50-odd minutes you spend eating to a gorilla's five hours of chewing every day. That's right, the great apes spend half their waking hours chewing. They also sleep a lot more than humans because chewing is hard work!

The chemical changes also make the process of digestion easier. Scientists theorize that they may have caused our intestinal track to grow shorter, as there was a lot less work to do. It could also have resulted in our brains getting larger! This interesting idea is still a hypothesis at this stage, and scientists are working on clues to understand it.

The biological change caused by cooking is the killing of bacteria and parasites, increasing the chances of human survival and prolonging the average human life to an almost unfair degree when compared to other species.

Hunter-gatherers Today

There are still a few hunter-gatherer tribes left in the world. The Kalahari Bushmen in Africa, the Sentinelese of the Andaman Islands, the Pirahã people of Brazil and the Aboriginal tribes of Australia are some of the tribes who continue to hunt animals and forage for food, relying solely on nature's resources for survival.

Most are fiercely protective of their privacy, such as the Sentinelese, who violently resist all contact from the modern world. And perhaps with good reason. While modern civilization collapsed during the devastating Indian Ocean tsunami of 2004, the Sentinelese survived, thus displaying superior survival skills compared to their civilized counterparts.

The Pirahã people are also wary of civilization, but they have allowed a few anthropologists to live among them and learn their way of life. They are known to be highly knowledgeable about the jungle, its animals and plants, what to catch, what to avoid, and how to survive. They do not store food, and they have no interest in farming. They just consume what they hunt and gather. Their sleep pattern is quite remarkable, and possibly a tool for survival – they take short naps throughout the day and night, lasting between 15 minutes and two hours at the most. They almost never sleep through the night.

The story goes that a century ago, two white Europeans, equipped with guns and all the latest survival equipment and food to last three months, set out on camels (six of them) to cross Australia from south to north. However, within a few weeks, their food ran out while they were in the middle of the desert. Luckily for them, a tribe of Aboriginals found them, fed them (with fish, fern cakes and roasted fat rats) and helped them on their way. Foolishly, however, one of the European men shot at the Aboriginals with his pistol, resulting in them fleeing and leaving the 'civilized' men to their fate. As it turned out, within a month of the departure of the Aboriginals, the men died of thirst and starvation.

In the very likely event that we run out of fuel and the natural resources that power our modern world, no prizes for guessing which group of people will survive!

THE ANCIENT CIVILIZATIONS

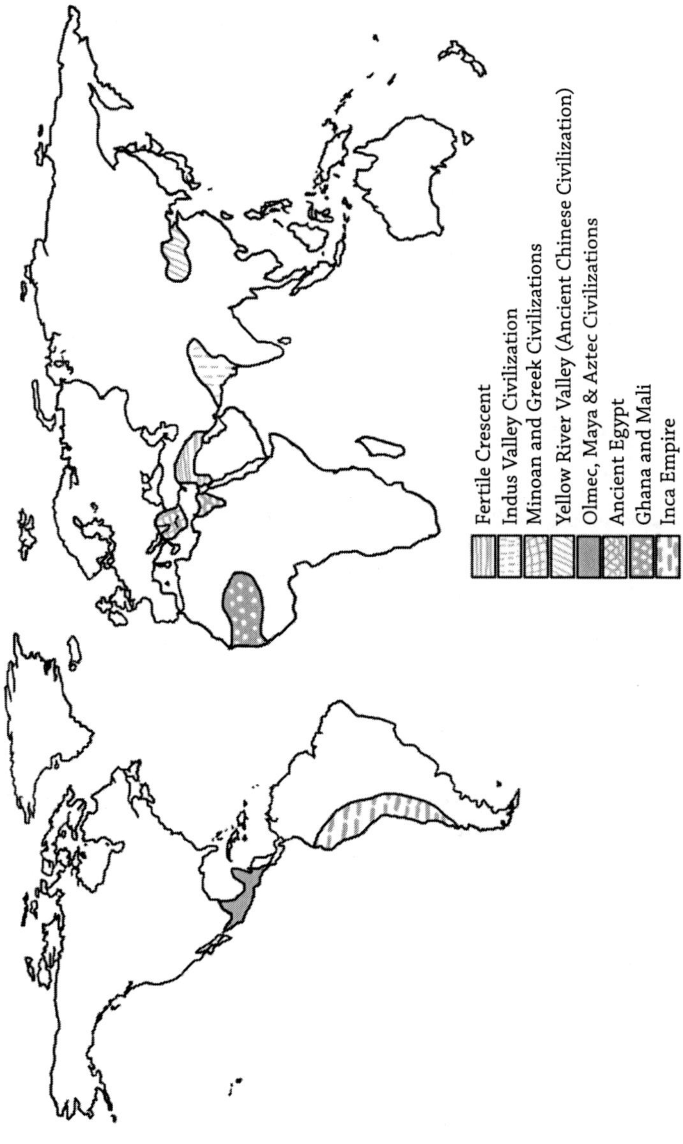

3

Playing with Clay

Riverbanks have always been good places for humans to establish settlements. One obvious reason is easy access to water. Another is the presence of clay.

Clay is great fun to play with! It moulds to any shape and keeps you occupied for hours. The earliest clay artefacts that archaeologists have found date back to 24,000 BCE. That's a very, very long time ago, perhaps even before or just at the time humans were learning to cultivate crops. These pieces of art have been found at a place called Dolní Věstonice in the Czech Republic. And someone must have had a lot of fun making them! They are small (4 to 5 inches) figurines of people, bears, lions, mammoths, horses and owls – none of them really practical. It appears that when humans first discovered clay and found that it could be shaped beautifully, they set about making toys. I say 'toys' because a fingerprint estimated to belong to a child between 7 and 15 years of age has been found imprinted on one of the figurines.

We can only hope that this child wasn't put to work to manufacture this artefact but was, instead, playing with it.

If you have played with clay (real clay, not plasticine) you probably know that water can wash away your masterpiece in less than half the time you took to create it. However, if you leave it out to dry in the sun, it becomes a little harder and lasts a little longer. The early humans figured this out, so once they made the clay figurines they put them into an oven (also known as a kiln) and baked them until they became hard.

When people learnt to build more efficient kilns that could retain heat long enough for the temperatures to exceed 1000° C, they discovered that clay became much harder and lasted for ages. This was probably when they started using clay to make utilitarian objects like pots, utensils and even pipes for plumbing. We wonder if they ever imagined that their creations would last more than 25,000 years!

Made in China

China is probably best associated with ceramics. Archaeologists have found pots dating back to 18,000 BCE in the Jiangxi province of China. These are, thus far, the oldest known pots in the world. They were probably made by rolling out clay in the shape of ropes and arranging them in coils to form pots. These were then baked in open fires or in simple kilns.

As the years progressed and skills developed, Chinese pottery became more intricate and decorative. Jade carvings, bronze inlays and lacquering can be seen in ancient Chinese pottery. In fact, delicate ceramic and porcelain cutlery is so deeply associated with Chinese culture that it is known as Chinaware. The pristine white cups and saucers are made from the earth near the Gaoling Mountains in China. Pottery from different parts of China varies greatly because of the different minerals mixed in the clay. The colours range from swirls of creams and greens to molten black glazes, translucent whites, deep purples and vivid blues.

Made in India

The most innovative use of clay in ancient times can be seen in the remains of the Indus Valley civilization. The cities of Mohenjo-Daro and Lothal had two-storeyed mud houses with possibly the world's first indoor plumbing. There were toilets inside the houses and terracotta pipes leading out of the toilets to reach the ground below. These pipes were connected to underground brick-lined sewers that opened out to the river estuary.

They made another clever use of clay – to sign or seal something. They did it with the help of a carved stone cylinder. When this cylinder was rolled on soft clay, it created a pattern. If someone possessed a stone with a unique design, this would act as their signature, maybe even used as a seal for documents.

Apart from pipes and seals, they also made elegant figurines out of clay. These artefacts were known for their finesse and were perhaps used for trade with other civilizations.

Made in Mesopotamia

The Mesopotamian civilization flourished roughly during the same time as the Indus Valley civilization, and its people have also left behind interesting clay objects, including seals, pottery, artefacts and clay tablets with writing.

But here's the most intriguing find of all – a toy found by archaeologists in the city of Sumer. It is a small animal with wheels instead of legs. A child could tie a string to this toy and pull it along. Why is this so interesting? Because at this point of time, there is no evidence of wheels being used for transport. Wheels, as far as evidence shows us, were only kept horizontally and used to make pots. But this toy had upright vertical wheels. So this could have been the beginning of an idea that wheels could be used for so much more than pottery!

4

Inventing the Wheel

2500 BCE, in the city of Kish in old Mesopotamia

Young Zimra was helping her father, Assur, gather red mud from the bank of the Euphrates. When they had gathered enough, they headed back home to Assur's little work shed in the corner of their yard. Father and daughter walked towards a wheel placed flat on the ground. Assur sat in front of the wheel and heaped the moist clay onto the centre. With his left hand, he gave the wheel a spin. And again. And again. It began spinning quite fast. With his right, he skilfully shaped the mass of clay into a flawless pot. Zimra never tired of watching this magical transformation.

But watch was all she could do. Assur never allowed her to actually make a pot. She was still too young. Assur caught the look of yearning on Zimra's face and smiled.

'Come here, I have something for you.'

From the back of the shed, Assur picked up a small clay object and gave it to his daughter. Zimra's eyes lit up when she saw that it was a little toy replica of her father's wheel.

She jumped up and got a little clay. She tried to make a pot on the miniature wheel, but either the wheel was too small or she was too unskilled, because the clay just collapsed into an untidy mess. She tried a few more times, but kept making bigger messes.

So Zimra gave up and shifted her attention to another toy, an old favourite – a little clay goat. It had been her constant companion for years and years, and she had played with it so much that its legs had worn off.

One afternoon she was lazing around in her yard. She dragged the legless goat toy along the ground, pretending it was walking. Out in one corner, she spotted the toy wheel, forgotten for many days. It was on its side, propped up against the wall. She extended her hand to grasp it. As soon as her fingers touched the rim, the wheel started gently rolling towards her. She was delighted with this new movement. Perhaps the wheel could be played with, after all!

A few minutes later, she ran to her father, breathless with excitement. 'Can you make me another wheel? Please?'

'What for? I am the best potter in Kish and even I have only one wheel!'

'Please, please, pleeeeeeeeeease?'

'Oh, all right, but only if you clean up the work shed for me tonight.'

The deal was struck, and Assur made another wheel. Zimra ran off with it to her play area at the other end of the yard.

Assur was curious. What did his daughter want to use a second wheel for? As he walked towards the play area, he saw her emerge from behind the wall with a totally new toy. It had a string attached to it, and Zimra was pulling it behind her.

'Where did you get that?'

'You made it for me!'

Zimra had attached the wheels to the body of the goat and was pulling the figurine by a string. Seeing the wheels upright and vertical was strange to Assur, who was used to always seeing them horizontally placed on the ground.

'It's not just the appearance that has changed but the function, too!' he exclaimed, looking at his daughter with pride. He knew this was an idea that would change the world.

The Rolling Wheel

It's quite astounding that the wheel – an object we associate with locomotion – was for centuries used only to make pots, as far as archaeological evidence suggests. Before the wheel was invented humans were already working with sewing needles, had constructed canals and had even crafted some complex musical instruments, like harps!

What is really interesting is that there are no real wheels in nature. There are beetles that can turn into a ball and roll forward; there are other beetles that lay their eggs in dung and roll that dung into a ball to transport their eggs; and there are tumbleweeds that are spherical and roll with the wind. But they are not really wheels. So, with nothing around them to draw inspiration from directly, it makes sense that humans took a few centuries to hit upon the idea that wheels could be used for transportation. Once they did figure this out, there was no stopping the journey of the wheel.

The wheel gradually became the key feature in every mechanical innovation. Think about it – every contraption, from a watch to a rocket, has a wheel in it somewhere. The simple wheelbarrow, the four-wheel drive, the Mars Rover, trains, steering devices, the pulley, the catapult, the cogs in a clock, the gears in an engine, the abacus, the mechanical calculator, water wheels, turbines, the Ferris wheel, the loom, the speedometer, the balancing scale, the conveyor belt... phew!

The earliest wheels were solid discs. Like a slice from a cylinder, rolling without control.

In fact, as early as 75,000 years ago, humans may have used boulders and logs to transport heavy objects, but this would have been effective only as long as the land was level and their destination was straight ahead of them. You couldn't possibly execute a turn with this contraption.

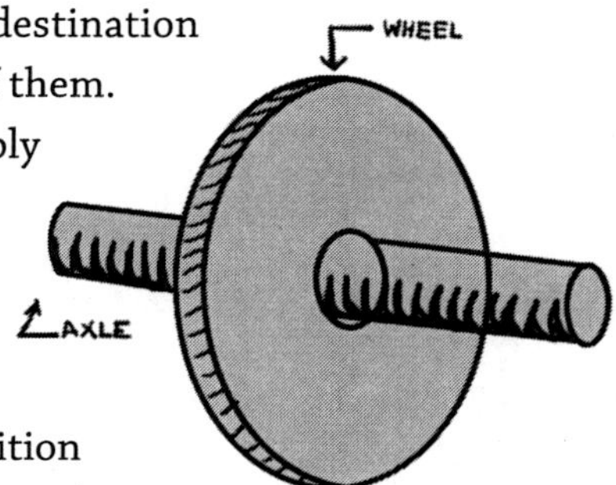

Then came the axle. This was the most important addition to the design that makes a wheel a wheel. The axle is a rod that passes through the centre of the wheel and the wheel must be able to rotate freely around it.

The wheelbarrow with a single wheel, pushed by hand, was one of the first innovations using the wheel-and-axle

concept. The earliest wheelbarrows have been found in Greece and China.

Around the same time came the idea of having spokes instead of a solid disc. Apart from making the wheel lighter, spokes also transfer the power from the hub to the rim, making the wheel move faster.

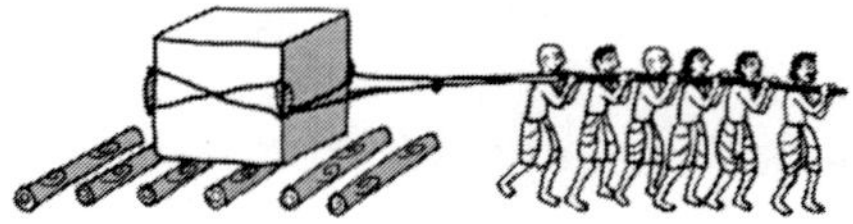

Early Uses of Wheels

Archaeological excavations in India, Rome, Egypt and Slovenia show spoked wheels dating back to the time period between 3500 and 1500 BCE.

These wheels were possibly used for chariots. Some have metal rims to maintain that perfect circular shape.

It is testimony to the power of the wheel that ancient civilizations that gave themselves wheels were the ones that left behind stupendous buildings and items of ingenuity for us to marvel at.

Is the Wheel Overrated?

But hold on, not *all* great civilizations used the wheel! The Maya people, who had established a powerful civilization in Meso-America had developed complex writing systems, advanced mathematics and astronomy, sophisticated art and architecture, and astute trade and commerce but did NOT use the wheel!

Well, that is not entirely correct – they did not use the wheel as a *transport* device. They had potter's wheels and looms for weaving, and also small animal figures with wheels (like pull toys), but they did not go beyond these uses. They even had paved limestone paths, and they probably used stone rollers to compact the roadbed, but no wheeled vehicle rolled down these lanes.

Why do you think that was?

One of the reasons is that their terrain was rugged and uneven, with narrow trails crisscrossing the area. Wagons did not work well there. It was probably more efficient to lug weights on your back than push it in an erratically moving wheelbarrow that you could not fully control.

Second, animals such as horses and donkeys, used to carry loads and pull wagons, were not native to Meso-America. Most civilizations that took the wheel to advanced uses were already using animal power for transport. Wheeled technology was only an extension of this use.

5

Smarty Pants

3200 BCE, in the city of Mohenjo-Daro in the Indus Valley

One bright, sunny day in the Indus Valley, a bright, sunny girl had an idea. She saw fluffy cotton growing on some shrubs and decided to observe more closely. She noticed that the fluffy ball was actually made up of many small fibres. And these fibres were not smooth and straight, but twisted and interlocked. When many fibres came together, they tended to intertwine around each other. She tried to separate them into individual fibres, but they held strong. So she put more fibres together and twisted them between her fingertips to make them stronger! She also observed that the longer the fibres, the stronger the hold.

This was exciting. She had just made thread!

Once she started, she could not stop. She kept drawing out more fibres and twisting them till she had a pile of thread at her feet. But wait, no, something wasn't right – the pile had become all jumbled and knotty.

It was too good an idea to give up on, just because of the tangled mess at her feet. She decided she had to make it work somehow. She had seen her mother winding her beautiful long hair around a smooth wooden stick to make it coil and sit in a pretty bun at the back of her head. If hair can be kept neatly in place by winding it around a stick, why not thread?

A simple stick inspired better designs and led to the spindle – a device that lets you pull out cotton fibres with one hand while winding them around the spindle with another. As the years passed, people came up with new and innovative ways of extracting cotton fibre to make thread.

And that's the thing with ideas – they tend to give rise to new ideas. If they are good enough, they survive. Like the iconic image of India's self-reliance – the charkha. Invented in the early 11th century, this nifty little contraption became a way for Indians to assert their self-reliance by making their own cloth.

The charkha has two wheels (big and small) and a spindle apparatus. The big wheel drives the smaller one, which in turn drives the spindle. A ball of cotton is carefully pulled and twisted around the spindle (with the left hand), while the big wheel is rotated with the right hand. Out comes thread!

Okay, so we have thread. How is that going to turn into clothing? Weaving, you say?

Mahatma Gandhi's Innovation

The bamboo charkha occupied a lot of space and was difficult to carry around. When Mahatma Gandhi was in Pune's Yerawada Central Jail, he put his time to good use by spinning his own thread. But he didn't stop there; he came up with an innovative addition to the charkha – the double-wheel drive, to allow for greater speed and control. It also made the charkha compact so that it could be folded into a box (either the size of a book or a briefcase) and carried anywhere.

While most of the Mahatma's ideas were abstract (ahimsa, truth, satyagraha), the charkha, and particularly his redesign of it, was a concrete and practical idea.

The charkha eliminated the need for India to be dependent on British textiles, and at the same time kinded the spark of self-reliance that was the key to winning us our independence.

The interesting thing here is that weaving was an idea that came up years before thread. Twigs, leaves and vines were interlaced to create shelters and fences. And they were not even first done by humans, but by birds and rodents to engineer their nests. Perhaps humans drew inspiration from these creatures as they used their fingers and looms to create a variety of useful things like ropes, mats and baskets.

Weaving is the process of interlacing horizontally and vertically arranged threads. The set of horizontal threads is called the weft and the set of vertical threads is the warp. When the warp and the weft are woven together, we have cloth.

Humans did not stop at weaving plain old cloth. Plant and vegetable dyes gave rise to colourful fabric. Most of these were earthen tones, like brown and orange. But in India, the native indigo plant produced a brilliant blue that was not found anywhere else in the world. It was in such great demand that it became a major unit of trade with other countries. Dyeing and printing took off from this point and became the major industry that it is today.

The Silk Route

Have you heard of how a Chinese princess discovered silk? The story goes that she was relaxing in her garden one day, sipping tea under a mulberry tree. Spotting some beautiful white cocoons on a leaf, she reached out to touch them. Oops! One of the cocoons fell into her hot tea. As she pulled it out, she saw that it unwound into one long silk thread. And that is how the luxurious fabric was born.

This may or may not be the truth, but essentially that is how silk is made. Just as cotton thread is drawn out and spun, silk thread is extracted by dunking silkworm cocoons in boiling water and drawing out silk thread.

It was lustrous, it was soft, it was nothing like anyone had seen before! Travellers from Europe and the Middle East were particularly enamoured, and a major trade was established. China guarded the method for many years, but a good idea can't be kept quiet for long. The secrets of silk manufacturing soon spread to India, which broke China's monopoly. Even five thousand years after its discovery, silk remains a symbol of luxury.

Otzi the Ice Man

Most of the conjecture in this book is based on bits and pieces of archaeological findings – a piece of loom here, a fragment of deerskin there. One lucky find was what is popularly known as Otzi the Ice Man.

While trekking along the Alps, a couple once came across a man completely covered in ice. They thought he must have been an unfortunate trekker who had slipped and got buried in the ice sometime back. They were right, but it was a little longer than 'sometime back'. It was just around five and a half millennia ago!

Because he was encased in ice almost as soon as he died, this man had been preserved remarkably well. Of particular interest to us at this point are his clothes. He was wearing leggings, a loincloth, a coat, a hat and shoes of some sort. First observations suggested that all these clothes were made from animal hide. A DNA study revealed that his coat was a patchwork of sheep and goat skin, the hat was made of bear fur and the shoelaces of cow hide. He had stuffed his shoes with grass for added warmth.

Winter Fashion in the Stone Age

Winter fashion during the Stone Age tended to be somewhat bulky, but practical considerations (like survival) put function above style. Layers were all the rage! Because the more layers you wore, the longer you lived. Animal hide was the material of choice, with the woolly mammoth's fetching rave reviews. Wolverine furs made the most stylish collars. And a draped bearskin was the preferred choice for a hoodie. Talons and claws made trendy accessories.

According to current archaeological evidence, around 45,000 years ago, it appears that someone hit upon the idea of making holes along the edges of two pieces of animal skin, passing a thin strip of skin through them and attaching them together – or, in other words, sewing. Holes were made using a pointed stone tool or perhaps even antlers and tusks. And they probably used strips of leather as cords to keep the pieces of animal hide firmly together, so that the 'garment' fit snugly around the body. This clever idea kept people warm and enabled them to move around in the cold, probably helping them survive the Ice Age.

The Ethics of Hunting

There was a time when it seemed like a good idea to use animals for human gains and comfort. Food was one reason, transport was another, as was labour for farming, and then, of course, there was clothing. Early humans hunted for survival and hunted only what was needed, perhaps because it was so difficult to hunt, with a very high probability of losing your life in the process. Viewed in this light, you could say it was ethical, as hunting was done only for survival.

However, humans then came up with weapons that could kill from a distance. And vehicles that could take them to safety. And armour that could protect them. Soon, industries started making hunting a business. It was no longer driven by the need to survive, but only by profit. Mink fur coats, for instance, became a fashion statement, and the process of manufacturing them cruel.

Humans also started hunting for pleasure and called it a sport. Big-game hunters would pose with a dead lion and call it their 'trophy'. In India, the maharajas and the British officers made it a national pastime and hunted the tiger to the brink of extinction. Seen in this context, hunting crossed all limits of ethics and decency.

When applied to labour and transport, it's a no-brainer – we have such sophisticated vehicles and machinery that it is simply criminal to use animals for these purposes.

Food is a moot point. While some argue that this falls within ethical boundaries, the methods of large-scale animal farming (keeping animals in confined spaces, not giving them space to move and so on) must definitely become kinder.

6

Give It in Writing

How did the idea of writing come about? Do you think it was a pressing creative urge, a fundamental human need to express lyrical thoughts and preserve them for future generations? The truth, as far as we have been able to decipher, is more mundane – it was a purely commercial need to keep accounts that led to the practice of writing!

3000 BCE, in the city of Uruk in old Mesopotamia

It was a busy day at the temple of Innana in Uruk, ancient Mesopotamia. The priests of the temple were the most powerful men in the kingdom. They controlled all the trade that happened in the region, whether it was a merchant from Anatolia (present-day Turkey) selling lamps or the local farmer trading his figs for some wool.

The priests had an efficient accounting system. They used clay tokens to represent every item being traded. A sphere for grain, a flat disc for sheep, an egg-shaped token for oil, a cone for wool and a cylinder for cattle.

Clay tablet listing food rations, around 3300 BCE

If a farmer brought in four sacks of grain, the accountant had to give four clay spheres as a 'receipt'. To keep them safe, a clay pot was first made, the tokens were sealed into it and then it was handed over to the farmer. If there were a hundred sacks of grain to be accounted for, they needed a hundred tokens.

Hmmm, doesn't sound so efficient now, does it? Imagine a super busy day. Lots of people have turned up, many with multiple bundles of items they are planning to trade. The chief accountant is getting nervous. Not just because of the number of people and all the merchandise, but also because he has brought along his eight-year-old son and has to keep an eye on him.

The clay artisans are sweating, trying to keep up with the demand to make tokens. A nobleman comes in with 12 sacks of grain, 17 bundles of wool and three cows. He is in a big hurry. He demands a receipt immediately. The accountants are trying to make him sit down and wait because making a receipt is quite a complicated task. First, the clay pot or *bulla* has to be prepared. Then they need tokens for each item he has brought in. So they need 12 spheres, 17 cones and three cylinders. These tokens will then be put into the clay pot. To prevent any tampering, the clay pot will be sealed.

There aren't enough tokens at hand. The artisans have just put their newly crafted tokens into the big furnace to bake and harden, but the nobleman is not willing to wait. He shouts at everyone, making them fumble and delay things even more. The chief accountant is trying to calm him down.

'The *bulla* is ready, as you can see,' he says, holding a still-fresh clay pot that is crumbling in his hand because it has not hardened yet, 'and we just need a few more tokens. As soon as they are ready, I will personally deliver the receipt to your home...'

But the nobleman keeps shouting. Scribes are flying in and out of the room, checking on the artisans' progress. The artisans' assistants walk in and out of the room, wanting to know how many more tokens are needed. The accountants get all muddled up, repeating the same numbers over and over again. The nobleman is now demanding to see the head priest!

Just then, some peasants come in, looking to barter their grain for temple sheep. They stand nervously, waiting for the chaos to subside. The chief accountant shouts at them, because he has no one else to shout at. The peasants shout back. The chief accountant wants to pull his hair out, so he hands over the soft clay *bulla* to the first person at hand – his eight-year-old son standing quietly by his side, taking in all the commotion with wide-eyed wonder.

Pot in hand, the little boy retreats to a corner of the chamber. He begins to press the soft clay between his palms until the pot turns into a flat disc of clay. Then he digs his fingernails in and makes little moon patterns. They look so pretty that he makes some more. Then the clay gets between his nails and skin, and this makes marking difficult. The shouting has got louder, and he doesn't like that. So he quietly slips out of the chamber. Outside, he picks up a dry twig and makes more markings on the clay. One of them looks like a cone. He tries making a circle, and then a cylinder. He is quite the artist! It takes him just a few moments to realize that if he made three cylinder marks, there would be no need to make the three cylinder tokens! Quickly, he makes more markings – 12 spheres and 17 cones to go with the three cylinders. The nobleman's receipt is ready.

Both clay *bullas* as well as flat clay tablets with 'markings' have been found at archaeological sites in what was the ancient city of Sumer in Mesopotamia (present-day Iraq). It can be surmised that once the practice of making marks on clay tablets took off, there was no need to make the tokens. Writing was born!

7

Following the Script

My name is Veena. You are reading this and can understand because you can read the script that I've used. What if you didn't know the script and I had to write down my name for you? I could use this picture:

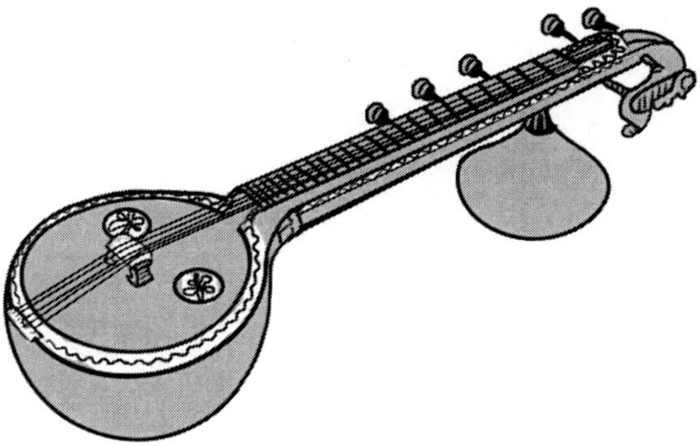

If you knew the name of this musical instrument, you would definitely be able to call me by my name.

Now, what about a different name? Like, say, Pinky?

I might split the word and go with two pictures:

PIN + KEY = PINKY

What I'm doing is creating a pictograph. This is how the ancient Egyptians and Mayans developed written communication. Their script was completely phonetic, with symbols representing voiced-out syllables of their language. The symbols are called hieroglyphs.

Chinese and Japanese characters are a little different. They use one written character expressing a word or a phrase. They are not phonetic. They are logograms.

Early writing in Mesopotamia used pictographs, but over time, it evolved into the cuneiform script. The cuneiform script was typically written on wet clay using reeds. These reeds are wedge-shaped at their ends. So the script has groups of wedge shapes to represent characters. In fact, so many bits of Sumerian writing have been unearthed that they span a period of 10,000 years, evolving from a simple token system of keeping records to a complex script that has been used to write famous poems like *The Epic of Gilgamesh*.

This idea of a phonetic script, where you could put down your abstract thoughts in a concrete (or terracotta) way, made it possible for writing to move away from merely representing physical items towards abstract concepts like feelings and ideas.

Similar changes were happening in other civilizations as well – in Egypt, Babylonia, China, Meso-America and the Indus Valley.

Egyptian hieroglyphs have been decoded, and we have been able to piece together the lives and culture of the Egyptian people because they decided to put it all down in writing.

However, the Meso-American and Indus Valley scripts have not been decoded yet, as very few samples have been found. So our idea of how their culture must have been is largely conjecture at this point in time.

The Rosetta Stone

The discovery of a rock with carved writing all over it was the key to understanding Egyptian hieroglyphs. Known as the Rosetta Stone, it contains a decree written in three different scripts – Hieroglyphic, Demotic and Greek.

Scholars familiar with the ancient Greek script were able to read that part alone. So they understood the edict. Using this, they tried to decode the other two scripts. It took them many years, but they did finally manage it, and now we know a good bit of Egyptian history because of this.

The Stupas

Ashoka's edicts were similarly carved on stone. They were written in Prakrit, a language long extinct. A British civil servant, William Jones, took it upon himself to study this language and understand the script. To do this, he first learnt Sanskrit, another ancient language that wasn't extinct. Combining that with his knowledge of local languages, he spent many years toiling over the script till he figured it out. And that is how we know the story of Ashoka and the Maurya dynasty.

8

Paper Trail

The writing of our ancestors rocked! There were Ashoka's edicts carved on rock, all the ancient Sumerian kings listed on a 4,000-year-old stone, the Maya hieroglyphs etched on temple walls, the letter that Claudius wrote on stone at the Temple of Delphi and so many other ancient writings that have survived to this day because the writers thought them important enough to carve into rock.

Carving out letters on rock is very hard work. If you want to compose the Mahabharata, for instance, with its over 2,00,000 lines, it might be difficult to keep the flow going while having to hammer and chisel your way through a rock face. If you make a mistake, you'll probably have to find a new rock, because 'deleting' or 'rewriting' is quite impossible!

So people started writing on wood, wax, leather, palm leaves, tree bark and papyrus. This made their task somewhat easier, and as a result they got a lot of writing done. However, there's a flip side to this – these materials are perishable, so very little of ancient literature written on these materials has survived. Only those works that were deemed to be important were copied and re-copied by generations of scribes, and that is how we have today parchments containing the Dead Sea Scrolls, the Egyptian Book of the Dead, the *Parameshvaratantra*, *Beowulf*, and other ancient pieces of literature.

The Dead Sea Scrolls are a collection of more than 800 manuscripts written on papyrus and animal skin. The earliest scrolls were written between the 3rd and 1st

centuries BCE. The contents range from law, religion and warfare strategies to directions to buried treasure!

The Egyptian Book of the Dead is the stuff horror movies are made of. It is a collection of instructions to the dead that detail the steps to be taken to successfully and safely navigate the afterlife. Believed to have been composed as early as 2300 BCE, it contains spells to be chanted during the funeral rites of the deceased.

The *Parameshvaratantra* is the oldest surviving palm-leaf manuscript. Dating back to the ninth century, it is a text on the philosophy of Shaivism, explaining the path to be taken by a devotee of Lord Shiva.

Beowulf is an Old English epic poem composed in the first century, full of kings and monsters and dragons. It is the original fantasy-adventure story that served as a source and inspiration for all other such books.

The scribes did not have an easy job. In India, for instance, the palm leaf was the preferred material to write on. But scribes couldn't just pluck a leaf off a tree and start writing. They had to 'season' it first. Palm leaves would be laid out to dry in the sun and then kept immersed underneath the silt in a pond for 15 days. Then they would be taken out, dried completely and have turmeric applied to the surface. Finally, they were ready to write on.

Sometimes the seasoning of the leaves was done by hanging them in a smoky area (like in the kitchen) for several days until they dried.

In some other places the palm leaves were carefully polished and then brushed with oil instead of turmeric – just a few of the many ideas people tried out to make leaves ready to write on.

But to write on with what?

Multiple options, it turns out. Scribes would use a pointed object (a stylus) to scratch on the surface and engrave the writing, or dip it in ink and let it flow on the surface.

Ink? How did they make that? Vegetable dyes? Indigo? Actually, the first forms of ink were made with lampblack, the soot left over from fire. Later, they used earth and mineral pigments that stayed longer than vegetable dyes or lampblack.

Palm leaf, Parchment or Papyrus?

The choice of writing material depended on the part of the world the writer was in. In India, the bark of the birch tree (found in the Himalayan region) was a popular surface to write mantras on. To use this, you had to first roll the inner bark gently off the tree. Even more gently, you had to set it to dry. This required great care if you didn't want to end up with broken strips in your hand! Then you'd boil it in water and lay it out to dry, finally coating it with oil so it would last longer.

In parts of Jerusalem, animal skin was the writing surface of choice. Rolled into very thin sheets called parchment, it was flexible and easy to work with.

In Egypt, scribes prepared papyrus using a laborious process. They first cut thin ribbons out of the interior of the Nile grass. Then they laid the strips side by side to make a sheet. They put a second layer of ribbons on top of this, but this time laying the strips at right angles to the first. Then they pounded the two layers together till they formed a single sheet. Papyrus is usually very strong, but repeated rolling and unrolling can cause the strips to come apart.

Ancient Chinese writers took writing to a new level when they used silk to write on! Smooth, light, durable and with a good capacity to absorb liquid ink, it was a great, if expensive, choice.

And Then There Was Paper!

Finally, we come to paper. To us, it is the most obvious choice of writing material, but it took a mixture of a few bright ideas to get there.

One idea involved the making of cloth using plant fibres such as cotton, flax, hemp and some grasses. Another contributing idea was using tree bark for writing.

Archaeological evidence suggests that it was in China that these two ideas came together. Samples of ancient paper have been found in China dating back to 200 BCE. The arid climate helped prevent the paper from decomposing. Even some of the ink on it remained visible!

This paper was probably made using hemp fibres soaked in water and pounded to a pulp using some sort of a heavy wooden hammer. This pulp would then be poured over a thin muslin cloth stretched across a frame. All the excess water would drip down, leaving behind a flat sheet of hemp-fibre paper.

People then started experimenting with other materials – bark from mulberry trees, bamboo, cloth rags, starch from rice and even fishing nets.

The Idea of Books

The first 'books' were papyrus strips or palm leaves tied together with string. They were very different from our idea of books. They were more like scrolls. The library in Alexandria in ancient Egypt had more than 5,00,000 scrolls in its collection! This was sometime during the third century BCE.

Some 400 years later, the Romans started writing on parchment. It was more flexible than papyrus and offered both sides for writing. Sheets of parchment were sewed in the middle, folded and even bound between wooden covers. Archaeologists call this a codex, the precursor to today's books.

They were not all written by hand, either. Almost every ancient civilization had some sort of printing block – made either of metal, clay or wood – which had characters printed in reverse so that when dipped in ink and pressed on paper, the writing would get 'printed'. This is known as block printing.

It was during the 14th or 15th century that one big idea changed the history of the book – the moveable type press. This was a nifty contraption that contained the entire alphabet of a language on individual blocks. You could arrange them into words, sentences or paragraphs, ink them and then press them on to the paper.

Why was this a history-changing idea? Because it eliminated the need for scribes to write out entire books by hand if they wanted to make copies. Books could now be replicated easily, and that is how the publishing industry was born and with it, authors and, indeed, readers.

9

Metallic Moments

Shiny and attractive, strong and versatile, metals have always fascinated humans. Even before humans discovered farming, agriculture, cloth, paper or writing, they knew how to extract metal from the ore and make useful little things with it.

This discovery took place in the days shortly after humans learnt to control fire – that is, starting it and stopping it at will, and making it flare up and simmer down to suit different purposes.

They must have had to play around with fire quite a bit before they mastered this skill. They would have discovered that digging a pit and letting the fire burn there makes it more intense, that is, makes it reach higher temperatures. Some objects, like dry twigs and charcoal, when put into fire, would have made the flames more intense, while some others, like rocks and stones, made no difference, and still others, like water, made the flame die out.

Imagine a prehistoric cave, outside which a shallow pit has been dug. Twigs are set on fire and once the fire reaches a medium intensity, some charcoal is added to raise the temperature. Maybe some other rocks get mixed with the charcoal. The prehistoric dwellers of the cave are trying to see exactly how hot this pit can get. They cover the pit, with the fire still burning, with a lid of loosely packed earth and grass. They know that air is needed for the fire to keep going, so they lift the lid just a little bit and blow air in using a reed. The continuous blowing keeps the fire going, and the charcoal ups the temperature. They've just made a furnace!

Is it hot enough to melt rock?

They decide to experiment. This greenish rock looks strange. It might produce an interesting result. They toss it into the fire and watch. At first, nothing happens. They shrug and just sit around the fire, drawing on the earth with twigs. Then they call it a day and decide to put out the fire.

As they pour water over the burning coals, they see something glowing. Wait, isn't water supposed to turn off the glow? But this isn't the glow of burning; it is the glow of something new!

The humans are excited. They let the rock cool and pick it up for more careful examination. They observe that bits of the greenish rock have turned pinkish yellow.

The next time, they crush the rock and toss it into the fire. They get even better results. The pinkish yellow substance melts out of the rock and coagulates into a shiny fist-sized mass.

This is no ordinary rock. It's called malachite and it is an ore. That is, it is a rock containing metal. In this case, copper. The very first metal mined!

Once these humans understand the basic process to start from, the possibilities become limitless. Tools are made, and that makes it possible to experiment further. Tongs, for example, make it easier to handle hot metal. Hammers can beat them into shape.

The Allure of Gold

What is it about this metal, more than any other, that has mesmerized humans across civilizations and cultures?

Gold artefacts, made more than 6,000 years ago, have been found intact and lustrous. Does that give you a clue?

Gold is non-reactive, does not corrode and is easy to work with. These qualities, along with its rarity, make it precious to humankind.

It is synonymous with 'treasure', has been looted, used as currency and collateral, pawned, used as a display of power, thought to have divine significance, crafted into delicate jewellery, woven into fabric, used in dental implants (yes, even ancient ones) and, in modern times, made into an investment, and used in electronic and aerospace equipment.

They mix different types of metals and make stronger new metals. They make alloys. They build furnaces. They extract more metal.

They build stronger weapons. And they build powerful civilizations.

The Rise and Fall of Lead

To begin with, everyone thought that using lead was a great idea. It was strong, easy to mould and abundantly available. From ancient times right up until the 1950s, almost everything – water pipes, paint, statues, kitchenware, weapons, gasoline, even certain medicines – had some amount of lead in it. Every industry used it to improve manufacturing efficiency and cut costs.

At some point during the 1950s, people began to suspect that all was not well. Groups of people in the same area or workplace started complaining of inexplicable aches, vomiting and hyperactivity. Animals were also seen behaving strangely, for no apparent reason. Careful observation revealed the common factor – lead. People working in lead factories were affected the most. As for the animals, the walls of their barns had been painted with lead paint, and when the animals licked the walls, they ingested lead.

Today we know that all the strange aches and weird behaviour can be attributed to lead poisoning. But back then, even after the circumstantial evidence was clear, the industry remained in denial. They conducted many experiments, desperately trying to prove that the cause was something other than lead, because many industries were heavily dependent on it. One of the company heads even drank a cup of lead to prove it was harmless. He knew it wasn't doing him any good, and he didn't go anywhere near this poisonous substance ever after. But that single cup was enough to do the damage – he died of lead poisoning. Still, companies continued to use it, simply because it was so profitable!

For 20 years people turned a blind eye.

Until scientific evidence was just too much to ignore. Governments finally woke up and issued laws to regulate the use of lead.

Here we pause for thought. The ancient Romans used lead to build their water pipes. At the height of their civilization, they had piped water in their homes. They also added lead into their drinks to make them sweeter. The story goes that their decline began when they grew complacent and partied more than they worked. But could there be another reason? Could lead poisoning have led to the fall of the great Roman Empire?

Here's another thought – not all ideas are good ideas!

Smooth Operator

Ancient metal artefacts are fascinating for the beauty and intricacy of their art, but one type of metalwork particularly stands out. It could be the iconic dancing girl figurine of Mohenjo-Daro, or the animal figurines decorating the tops of pins in ancient Mesopotamia, or the astonishingly complex bronze artefacts found in caves in Israel, and much later, hollow seamless celestial spheres crafted in Mughal India and parts of Europe.

This is a type of metalwork that uses no hammering, welding, fixing or fusing of any sort. The object is completely smooth, with not a single mark, scruff, or joint anywhere on its surface.

The artists who made these used a brilliant technique called lost-wax casting. For this, the potter and the metal worker have to work together. First, a model is carved in beeswax. It is then coated with clay, and heated. This causes the clay to harden, and the wax to melt. After the wax has completely melted, you are left with a clay mould into which you can pour molten metal, and out comes your artefact!

10

Money Matters

If I have an apple orchard and you have a wheat farm, I will at some point have more apples than I need, and you will have more wheat than you can consume. So we decide to trade. We fix the quantities to be traded in a way we think is fair: a few kilograms of apples for a few kilograms of wheat. This is called barter.

But what if the apples are not ready at the same time as the wheat? You bring in many sacks of wheat, but only half my apples are ready to harvest.

Remember those clay tokens back in Mesopotamia? Well, I could make some tokens, I suppose, as a sort of pledge that I'll hand over the rest of the apples to you when they are ready. Maybe I'll make one token for every sack I owe you.

Then there's that expert fence maker. I had asked her to repair a part of my fence with some strong bamboo. She turned up the same day as you. I have no apples, so I'll make her some tokens too. A week later she says she gave the tokens to the potter as she needed some pots, so she tells me to give the apples to the potter.

Then things get chaotic. Everyone starts making clay tokens of shapes and sizes and designs of their choosing, mixing them all up till no one knows what the tokens mean anymore. So the kings decide to take matters into their own hands. They make coins.

It was in a place called Lydia in Asia Minor (modern-day Turkey) that the oldest coins (so far) were found. Estimated to be around 2,700 years old, these coins were made from a naturally occurring blend of gold and silver called electrum. The coin bears the image of a roaring lion on one side and has a punch mark on the other side. It must have been handmade using a die cast and an anvil.

Lydia was an important trade hub, connecting the Asian kingdoms to the Greek cities. It is no wonder that the idea of making coins originated there.

There's a lot of precision involved in making money. First, it can't be any old thing that anyone can make. Because, then everyone will end up having money, but that money would be worthless precisely because everyone has it. Money has to be earned. Only then is it worth something.

When humans thought of making coins, they chose gold and silver for exactly these reasons. They were scarce, so not everyone could make their own. They were weighed precisely so that a proper value could be established for all the denominations. In the Rig Veda, there is a mention of different types of coins – *nishka*, *suvarna*, *shatamana*, *pada* – and they were all weighed against a shiny red seed called the *gunja*.

Cowrie Shells

Most island cultures around the world have used seashells (particularly cowrie shells) as currency. Some believe they started the practice of collecting and valuing these shells from as far back as the New Stone Age. This continued till the early 20th century. They worked pretty well too. Better than clay tokens for a number of reasons. For one thing, no one could make them – they had to be found. A bit like gold! They were attractive, so people started wearing them as neckpieces. They were hard and durable, too. They came in different sizes, so you could have different denominations.

Paper Money

Our era, that is, the history of four or five of our preceding generations, has been dominated by money in the form of paper.

Why paper?

It's flimsy, not precious, doesn't withstand wear and tear and lends itself to being counterfeited unless elaborate security measures are taken.

Why did people think it was good idea?

As it turned out, it wasn't. We'll soon get to the reasons.

But why did they do it in the first place?

During the seventh century CE, China was a very prosperous place. Trade was booming. Lots and lots of coins were required for transactions. The counting was tiresome. So the people of China came up with innovations to deal with this – like coins with a hole in the middle so that many of these could be strung together. They had specific lengths of string that could hold, say, 10 or 100 coins, so there was no need to count them out every time. But the big problem was that it all got terribly heavy. Sometimes the currency weighed several times more than the commodity being traded!

Well, by this time, China had invented paper. They found a solution to the coin problem – they just drew the number of coins on the paper and used that as a record of payment.

Sounds like a neat idea, right?

Except that soon, everyone started making paper money and it stopped being precious anymore! The sellers would look very silly when they demanded a higher price for precious goods, and all the buyer had to do was draw coins on a piece of paper. Merchants didn't want to sell anything. So buyers were left drawing worthless circles on paper. Before they realized it, China was facing a full-blown economic crisis.

Because of this, China stopped paper money entirely and restarted it only in the modern era when enough control and security was put in place. This is why people can't just print their own money.

11

Through the Looking Glass

Lightning strikes again. It's a stormy night, very similar to the one that occurred a million years ago near a damp, dark prehistoric cave...

Except this time it is not close to a prehistoric cave, but out on a beach.

And there are no trees, so lightning comes straight down to earth and strikes the sand. One billion joules of energy hit the sand, reaching temperatures of 2500° Celsius, and melt the sand into liquid.

And because lightning only lasts a fraction of a second, the sand cools almost immediately. The liquid solidifies rapidly, resulting in a fused mass of silica called fulgurite, also known as glass.

Perhaps someone went exploring on the beach the next day and found a strange, beautiful substance in the sand. A tubular structure with a network of delicate

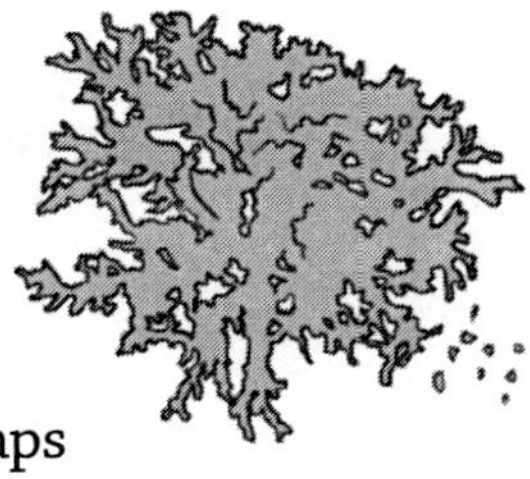

white strands coming out of it. Perhaps they had seen the lightning strike. Perhaps they figured out that lightning produces extreme heat, and that causes the sand to turn into glass. Perhaps they tried to replicate it. Perhaps they were not successful at first. Because the minimum temperature required to melt sand is 1800° Celsius. And only a furnace can do that. Open fires or even fires in a pit can't do that. Perhaps they just kept the fulgurite and told the story of the lightning to their descendants, and when their descendants made a furnace that could reach high temperatures, they tried to melt sand in those. Perhaps they succeeded, and that's how we have glass today!

Lightning strikes on sand don't happen very often. And fulgurite is formed quite deep below the surface, so one would have to dig to get it. This is why naturally made glass is quite rare. And this is why we imagine that it may have taken many generations to hit upon the idea that heating sand can create a beautiful new substance called glass.

Once humans understood how to make this new substance, they didn't start making bowls and glasses overnight. They started with beads. Colourful glass beads have been found in many ancient sites (Indus Valley, Mesopotamia and Egypt) around the world dating back to between 3500 and 1700 BCE. They also made beautiful glazes on clay pottery.

The breakthrough came when someone figured out that you could blow glass while still molten to make useful shapes like bowls and vases. From there, the ideas just kept rolling. Decorative trinkets, exquisite goblets and glasses, bottles, lamps and weapons were some of the first objects people made.

The First Glass Factory

A remarkable glassmaking unit was discovered in Phoenicia (present-day Lebanon, Israel and Syria). It is the oldest glass factory that archaeologists have found. The Phoenicians may have been the first to use glass blowers to create containers. It appears that they used an iron pipe, 1 to 2 metres long, with a sort of holder at one end that kept the molten glass in place. The glassmaker blows through the pipe while the molten glass on the other end expands like a bubble. The interesting thing is, this is pretty much the same technique used today.

Ingredients in Glass

We humans never leave a thing alone. We like to mix things up, do something different, add some ingredients, take some out and see what happens. We call it experimentation. And it leads to new and improved versions of things. This kind of experimentation led to some very useful discoveries in glassmaking. The ancients found out that adding soda (sodium carbonate) to sand (silica) made it melt at a lower temperature. Adding lime (calcium oxide) stabilized it so it wouldn't melt away altogether. And lead oxide made it remarkably clear.

Copper was great for making coloured glass, especially green and ruby red. Copper oxide and cobalt oxide gave glass a nice shade of blue. Iron turned glass greenish, while manganese made it yellowish.

For sparkle, the decorative kind of crystal glass, lead makes a good additive. The more the lead content, the sparklier the glass.

For correcting the vision, lanthanum oxide is the additive of choice. This increases the refractive index of the glass, making it suitable for optical lenses.

For using in ovens, boron is added to glass so that it can withstand very high oven temperatures.

Windows

When you think of windows, what comes to mind first? Glass panes, surely? You may be surprised to know that even a thousand years after humans started making glass objects, windowpanes were non-existent. People used paper to cover their windows or just made intricate lattice designs that let light in while providing some amount of privacy. This is because flat glass is quite difficult to produce. The ancients managed to create intricate art with glass, some of which was quite tricky to make, but not flat panes.

But why is it so difficult to make flat glass? It's because glass is a strange state of matter – it is neither liquid nor solid, but an amorphous solid. Well, it feels solid, right? Why isn't it a solid? Because the atoms in solids are arranged in neat regular rows that give them their rigid shape. Glass atoms are disorganized. They are so because glass is made by first melting silica and then rapidly cooling it to a 'supercooled' liquid, and then further cooling it till it gets a solid rigidity. But its atoms never really line up neatly, so it settles into an amorphous solid.

Before it settles into its amorphous solid state, it needs to be shaped. Glass bowls are easy to make because they can be blown. But to make flat panes, people had to try out different ideas. Some poured the molten glass into a mould. When they did this, it came out with one matte surface and the other glossy. So they tried blowing the molten glass while simultaneously flattening it with a wooden mallet. This caused it to become lumpy.

Some tried a more complicated method, such as blowing the glass, opening the end opposite to the blowpipe and spinning it vigorously. The centrifugal force would cause the glass to flatten out into a disc. Magic? Not really. If you hold a small object in your hand and spin and spin, and at some point let it go, it flies outwards from you. Something similar happens to glass as it is spun while molten. It spreads outwards and shapes itself into a disc.

Another method that worked well was to blow the glass into a cylindrical shape and use a metal tool to cut it open lengthwise, so that it opens into a rectangle. With some skilful heating and cooling, it can be flattened out to make a pretty good-looking glass pane.

Mirrors

Mirrors could be made only after the art of making flat panes of glass was mastered. Glass mirrors, that is.

Not that people never looked at their own faces before this. They used polished metal surfaces and, of course, the clear surface of a pool of water.

Those living in volcanic areas had an advantage. Sometimes, the lava from erupting volcanoes would generate so much heat that the rocks would melt and rapidly cool to form a glass-like material called obsidian. When polished, this material acquires a reflective surface, making a sort of mirror.

While a pool of water is a good reflective surface and polished metal is great too, glass, at first glance, seems like a rather poor choice to make a mirror out of. You can see right through it! It is, therefore, surprising that someone would think of making a mirror out of glass. More so when you consider that the early glass that people made tended to be uneven and, when coated, would produce a distorted image.

In spite of this, at some point during the first century BCE, someone in Phoenicia hit upon the idea of coating one side of glass with an amalgam of silver and mercury. Though not a perfect reflection, the result must have been encouraging enough for them to continue with this experiment, until, years later, a perfectly straight mirror was coated with a perfectly reflective material and the perfect mirror was made.

12
To the Stars

When something occurs repeatedly, in a pattern – like day and night, how winter is always followed by summer, the phases of the moon – you start suspecting that something is going around in circles.

At first glance, it seems likely that the sun is going around the earth. It sinks every evening and rises from the other side every morning, right?

Deeper observation of the night sky, however, tells you a different story. If you live in the northern hemisphere and observe the night sky in, say, December, you will see Venus shining brightly most evenings and constellations such as Orion, Gemini and Taurus, to name a few. In June, however, you will see a different pattern in the sky, most visibly the constellations Aquila, Cygnus and Lyra, and the planet Jupiter. But the next December, you will see the same planet and constellations you saw last December. This is a pattern. A cycle that repeats.

What can we make of this?

Imagine you are on a carousel. As your seat goes past your parents, they wave at you, and you wave back. Then you see other people as the carousel takes you on a circular path. When you complete a full circle, there – you see your parents again.

Observe any similarities with the constellations you see?

The ancient Indian astronomer Yajnavalkya (living in the ninth century BCE) probably spent many years gazing at the beautiful night sky and observing its patterns. He wrote in the *Shatapatha Brahmana*: 'The sun strings these worlds – the earth, the planets, the atmosphere – to himself on a thread.' In the third century BCE, Greek astronomer Aristarchus also said something similar, and worked out some mathematics too to back up his theory. But back in those days, no one took them very seriously because our observation 'clearly' tells us that the sun is moving!

So for centuries, people believed that the earth was at the centre of the universe.

Let the Stars Be Your Guide

Our ancestors spent a lot of time looking at the stars, their changing patterns and some *un*changing patterns, and came up with one spectacular idea that changed the world.

They learnt to navigate using the stars as their guide.

They observed how certain constellations were visible only in summer and others only in winter. Just like the sun, they seemed to set and rise, but so much more slowly, taking months to do so. They observed how some constellations were visible throughout the year. They also noticed one star in particular that didn't seem to move at all.

This is Polaris, or the North Star. And the constellations that are visible throughout the year appear to rotate around this star (only from the northern hemisphere, though).

So, if you're standing at the North Pole, Polaris will be directly overhead. At the equator, Polaris will be over the horizon. If you're anywhere in between, the North Star will be somewhere between the horizon and over your head.

The angle between Polaris and the horizon can help you estimate where you are. In other words, you will know your current latitude. You could use an instrument called a sextant to measure this angle. (It would show you 90 degrees at the North Pole and zero degrees at the equator.) But if you don't have a sextant, use your fists for an approximation. Extend your fists straight in front of you with the knuckles facing outwards. Then extend one hand and put that fist on top of the other. This way, fist over fist, work your way up from the horizon to the North Star. Each fist is approximately 10 degrees. If it takes you three fists, you are at 30 degrees latitude. If you are in India, it would probably take two and a half fists. You are at 23 degrees latitude, the Tropic of Cancer.

But you could be anywhere along the Tropic of Cancer. How do you know whether you are in India or Mexico?

With just the stars, you can't know. But you can tell whether you have been travelling eastwards or westwards.

You need to observe a star that sets in the east and rises in the west. Note down the time it sets and rises every evening. If it rises earlier every evening, then you are heading east. By keeping track of how much earlier, you can tell how far east you have travelled.

Stars to Watch Out For

To navigate properly, you need to know at least 38 constellations and 56 stars.

But if you aren't planning to discover a new land or circumnavigate the earth all by yourself, you can get by with knowing only the ones that really stand out.

If you are in the northern hemisphere, you can first locate Polaris, and then try and spot these constellations:

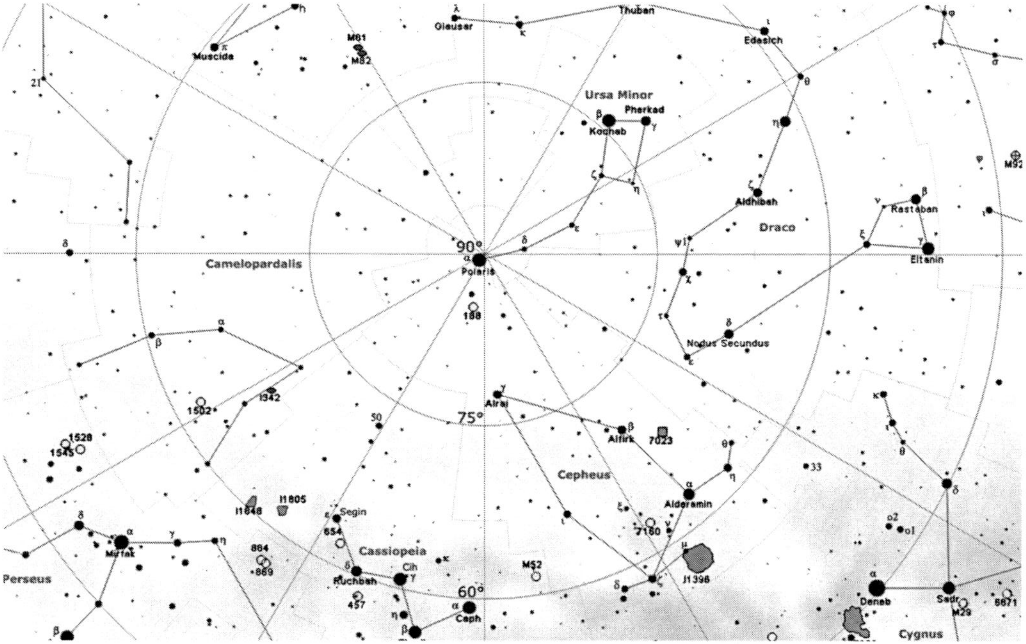

If in the southern hemisphere, locate the Crux and then look for these constellations:

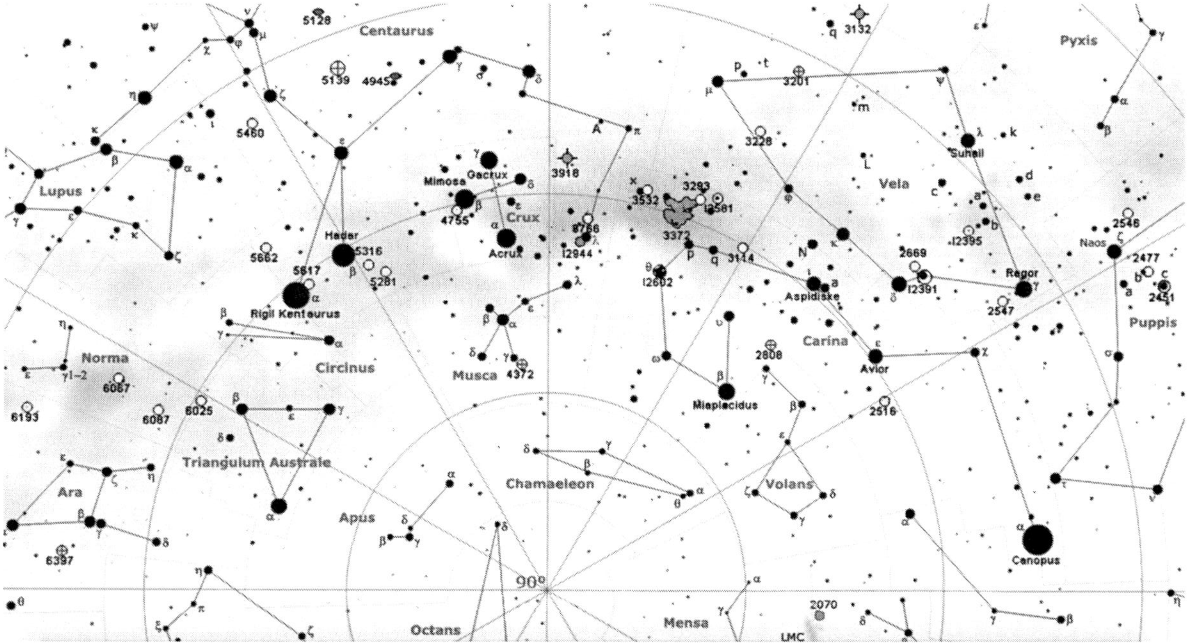

13

The Sound of Music

Do you come up with a tune first, or the words? Does the harmony have to fall in place first, or should the lyrics fit the metre? When you hum a tune, do the notes dance in your head or do you hear the words of the song?

Birds sing. Do they have words? A mother croons to her baby. Do her words make sense to anyone else? What came first? Songs or music? Notes or words?

We don't know. We may never know. So, let's just get something to eat. Preferably something prehistoric. Like this meal that little Ug was nowhere close to finishing.

20,000 years ago, somewhere on prehistoric earth

'Finish your dinner, Ug,' said Ug's mother. Not in those words, exactly, maybe not in words at all but with sounds and gestures (like a thwack on the head) that effectively got the message across.

Ug looked at his half-eaten bird's leg with disgust. Then he saw his mother walk into the deeper part of the cave, where she stored all the stuff. Quietly, he sneaked out of the cave, to that cute little wolf cub that had followed him home last evening. He gave the bone to the cub, who cleaned it up in a way that would make Ug's mother happy.

Ug and the cub then started playing with the bone. Ug was surprised to see that the bone was completely hollow. This was different from the bones of the other animals he had eaten – they were all filled with marrow. He blew through it, and the soft whistle made the wolf cub's ears perk up.

Ug extended the bone towards the wolf cub, who eagerly grabbed it in his mouth and started playing with it. His sharp canine made a hole in it.

'Oh no!' Ug didn't want it broken. It was a beautiful hollow bone. He took it back and tried to blow into it again, hoping the soft whistle would still sound good.

You know what? It sounded better! He tried blowing through it from different angles, vertically and horizontally, and was delighted with all the different sounds he heard.

Then he ran into the deeper part of the cave, straight to the sharp tool his mother used for chipping into the rock surface. He wasn't allowed to use it, so he had to make sure she wasn't looking when he swiped it. Quickly, he took it outside, where the wolf cub was expectantly waiting. It seemed to the cub that something exciting was about to happen.

Ug used the chipping tool to make a few more holes. He spent the entire day blowing through the holes, closing one, then the other, experimenting and creating all sorts of delightful sounds.

Ancient Flutes

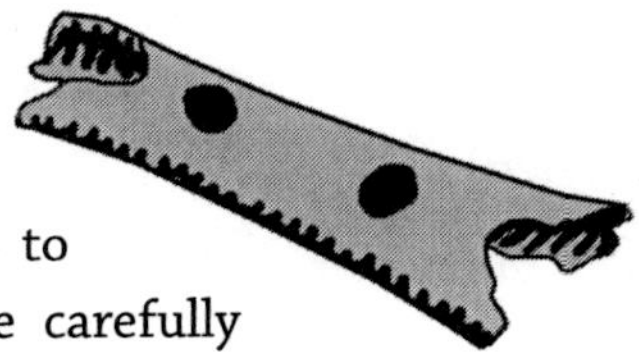

This picture is that of a fragment of vulture bone found in a prehistoric cave in Germany. It is estimated to be 30-40,000 years old. The carefully rounded holes and even spacing strongly indicate that it was human-made and a flute, although scientists are always trying to rule out the possibility that some animal might have gnawed through it. It does seem highly unlikely that an animal would gnaw holes spaced so melodically apart!

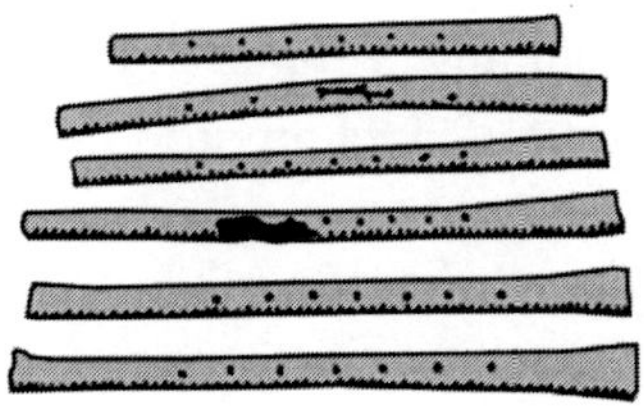

This is a picture of a set of flutes found in China. They are estimated to be around 9,000 years old. There is no doubt that they are flutes, each having seven holes and a smaller eighth on the other side, possibly to allow for pitch corrections.

These prehistoric flutes with seven notes are technically the same as those made today!

Rock Music

A lithophone is a rock on which some clever chiselling has been done, so that it produces music when tapped.

A 2,500-year-old 'ringing' rock has been found in a village called Anjetti in southern India. This rock has close to a hundred pieces 'scooped' out of it smoothly. When scientists took another stone and lightly struck these scoops, a ringing sound was produced. Could it have been an ancient musical instrument? Scientists are still in the process of figuring it out.

In relatively more recent times (a thousand or so years ago) a large hall in the Vijaya Vittala temple in Hampi (which was part of the Vijayanagar Empire) was built with musical pillars. There are a few large pillars surrounded by several smaller pillars, constructed as simple circular columns without any carvings. When lightly tapped, these pillars produce melodic tones, turning the whole temple into one giant musical instrument. Several other temples in south India (Madurai Meenakshi temple, Nellaiyappar temple and the Alwar Tirunagari Temple, to name a few) also have such musical pillars.

14

Picture Perfect

20,000 years ago, in little Ug's cave on prehistoric earth

Little Ug was sitting against the wall of his cave. His father was trying to tell his mother all about some adventure he had that morning. He was making a lot of guttural sounds and gesticulating with his hands, but it was clear that Mother didn't really get the enormity of what Father had gone through. She was stirring the large pot of stew and nodding absentmindedly, completely unimpressed. Ug didn't understand his father either. He had a piece of charcoal and was scratching with it on the cave floor. Father was getting frustrated.

Put that charcoal away and listen to me! he wanted to say, but he had no words for that, being a caveman in the Later Stone Age. It came out as angry growling sounds – 'UGG GRRR GGGG UGUGUGRRR GRRR' – while he stomped over to where Ug was sitting in order to snatch up the piece of charcoal and throw it away.

Just as his fingers were about to grip the charcoal, something made him stop and stare. Ug had made a few scratching marks – lines and dots and curves – but it seemed to fascinate his father. Excitedly, Father took the piece of charcoal and ran over to the wall of the cave that was illuminated by Mother's cooking fire.

He started making deft strokes. His hand moved so fast and so passionately that Mother and Ug stopped what they were doing and watched the lines take shape on the wall.

Ug recognized it at once! A most dangerous creature. All other creatures, especially ones like him who lived in caves, ran away as soon as they saw that creature. It could uproot trees with just one powerful push from its enormous forehead. Two large tusks completed the task if the tree was huge and deeply rooted. Each of its legs was bigger than ten strong people put together and that long nose was pure muscle. It was a giant mammoth.

Father then drew a small stick figure facing the mammoth. He pointed to it, and then to himself.

'Yuuuuuuuuhhhh!' said Ug, understanding that his father had drawn himself.

'Mhhhrrrmmm!' replied Father with satisfaction.

He then drew himself holding what looked like a bow. He added arrows sticking out of the mammoth. Finally, he drew about half a dozen stick figures lying on the ground.

Mother's eyes had grown big and round. She knew now exactly what had happened. Father had killed a giant mammoth. The biggest creature on earth. Everyone else with him had died. He had managed to kill the mammoth with just a bow and arrow. (It might have helped that she had discovered a deadly poison the previous month and had told him to dip his arrow heads into it.)

This picture was certainly worth a thousand words.

Colours and Brushes

Early cave art was monochrome – charcoal mixed with spit or animal fat. Then the early humans discovered that hematite (iron oxide) was a source of rich red pigment. So we started seeing art in two colours – carbon black and red ochre. Clay was a good source of yellows and blacks. Ground calcite was used to make white pigment. Prehistoric caves on every continent on earth (except Antarctica) contain art. So far, most of these cave paintings have been found in Europe (particularly France), and some caves even seem to have been used as art galleries.

Rock painting found in Bhimbetka, Madhya Pradesh

Indian cave paintings, even back then, were more colourful than most. They used shades of purple, green and brown in addition to the standard black and red.

Cave paintings are very sophisticated in execution. They show remarkable strokes and brush skills. Some cave artists seemed to have made preliminary sketches by carving an outline on the rock face, while others jumped right into painting.

Some applied the pigment with their fingers, or used leaves or moss to dab the colour.

Cave painting found in Lascaux, France

Over time, they created brushes with animal hair.

There are some paintings that look like they have been done using spray paint! How did they achieve that?

Archaeologists think they may have blown pigment through hollow bones or reeds straight on to their rock canvas.

I am tempted to say what a long way we have come from there in terms of art, but one look at these cave paintings and it seems as though we reached the pinnacle when we started!

15

Friends Forever

20,000 years ago, just outside little Ug's cave on prehistoric earth

Ug's little wolf cub was cute and playful. Ug's parents were initially not very happy about having a baby wolf around them – wolves were dangerous creatures and the cub's parents might come looking for him. But this cub was adorable, and they could not help falling in love with him. The cub had adopted Ug's family as his own, accepting Ug's father as the leader of the pack and Ug as his best friend. Ug made a drawing of himself and the little wolf on the wall of his cave.

Soon, some other wolves began approaching the humans. They were attracted by the scraps of meat and bones thrown in the rubbish dump. The humans had mixed feelings about this. If the wolves showed any signs of aggression, they would have to drive them away. But the milder ones were useful to have around. They learnt obedience and developed an unquestioning loyalty, and were useful in keeping other dangerous animals at bay. Some humans began taking them along on hunting trips. They turned out to be excellent hunting partners, as their speed, ferocity and instinct for danger worked well with human ingenuity. Together, they became unbeatable.

Thousands of years later, Ug's descendants had built a proper settlement in the area. They had cleared the trees, built huts, dug a well, planted crops, established clay-making centres and had a nice little civilization going.

There were still ferocious wild wolves in the jungle surrounding the village. And the humans were still afraid of them. But they had reliable protectors – dogs! Descendants of Ug's little wolf cub, these dogs looked very different from their ancestors. They had floppy ears compared to the perked-up triangular ones of wolves, shorter snouts, smaller teeth and paws, and curly tails. They even made barking and woofing noises as if they wished to say something. Wild wolves, on the other hand, rarely bark.

Over time, dogs evolved into a separate species. Indeed, no one thought to make a connection between wild wolves and their pet dogs, but somewhere, deep inside a cave covered with bushes and thorns, there was a small drawing of a little boy and his wolf cub, telling a different story.

The Taming of the Dog

A 60-year-long experiment with foxes (that are different from yet related to wolves and dogs) produced some interesting results. Researchers in Russia domesticated 40 generations of foxes to understand how dogs become domesticated. They began the process of taming by feeding the foxes and getting them used to human company. As the foxes' interaction with humans increased, some of them displayed less aggression, like biting, while others remained indifferent and a few continued being hostile. So the researchers selected only the tamest ones to breed and they continued the experiment with the offspring of the tame foxes. With successive generations, surprising things happened – some foxes developed mottled or spotted fur and started looking visibly different from their ancestors. Their ears began getting floppy, their tails curved and their snouts more rounded. But here's the most important change – they seemed to understand humans, or at least, interpret human gestures such as pointing. The experiment is still going on, and so far, the foxes do not respond to human speech, the way dogs do.

But then, dogs have spent a lot more time with humans than the foxes in this experiment have. With tens of thousands of years of being together, dogs and humans have had plenty of time to take their relationship further, establishing the best kind of friendship there can be between species!

How Dog Breeds Evolved

It can be difficult to imagine that a Chihuahua and a Great Dane share a common ancestor. Yet, DNA analyses point to this truth.

Think about it: humans and houseflies too share a common ancestor, as do all living creatures, having descended from a single-celled organism all those billions of years ago. When we consider that wolves evolved into dogs over a period of tens of thousands of years, it seems plausible that German shepherds and poodles diverged from a common ancestor a few millennia ago.

The other thing to note is that the domestication of wolves took place in many different places of the earth, and over the years, dogs developed characteristics to suit that environment, becoming native to that particular place and not appearing in others. For example, the St Bernard has adapted to cold climates and thrives in alpine habitats. The Mudhol (or caravan hound) is a dog that was bred in the Mudhol region of India specifically as a hunting companion and is not found anywhere else in the world. In places where sheep were reared, 'herding' dogs, such as Alsatians and collies, evolved.

Some dogs, such as golden retrievers and Irish setters, were bred specifically to be hunters' companions in Victorian England.

More recently, we have dogs for search-and-rescue missions, sniffing out bombs, mobility assistance, medical alerts or, simply, companionship.

As for Chihuahuas, they were bred to keep tarantulas out of houses in Mexico!

Once humans established themselves as the leaders of the pack, it was easy to tame wolves and domesticate them, leading to the evolution of the dog. Humans used the same idea to domesticate other animals. Wild sheep, prized for their wool, were soon herded into flocks, with a human taking on the role of the leader. Sometimes dogs were used as lieutenants. Soon, goats and pigs also came under human command. They all went through a process of evolution over thousands of years and evolved into the species they are today. Some of them still exist in their wild form, such as wild pigs, showing us that there could have been wild counterparts for most domesticated species.

One act of domestication, however, resulted in the mutation of not only the animal but also us humans.

A very long time ago, much before the wheel was invented, there roamed in the wilderness of the Indian subcontinent the aurochs.

An aurochs looked like an ox, except it was much larger, standing six feet tall at the shoulder! And it weighed no less than a ton. Taller than the average human and weighing a lot more, how could anyone think this was a candidate for domestication? Herding sheep or throwing a bone to a wolf cub is a completely different game.

Aurochs skeletons have been found with marks of wounds from arrows. So we know that they were probably hunted for their meat. We could then conjecture that a wounded aurochs or its young ones could have first entered human circles. And that isn't the end of the story. It probably took humans many generations to truly domesticate an aurochs from the imposing wild animal it was to a docile cow. Note that 'domesticate' here doesn't mean 'tame'. Elephants can be tamed, but they are still wild. But wolves and aurochs were domesticated to such an extent that their genetics were altered and they evolved into a new species.

Humans began to depend on aurochs more and more for farming, food, hide and milk. Milk, most importantly, had a role in transforming us. The early humans never drank milk after infancy. However, when cows were domesticated and we developed a taste for milk, our bodies changed to accommodate this new food. There are still some humans who cannot digest cow's milk. They are lactose intolerant. All early humans were lactose intolerant, but because of our liking for and dependency on milk and milk products, the gene that determines lactose intolerance grew recessive.

So the next time you wrinkle your nose at that glass of milk in the morning, you can blame it on your prehistoric ancestors!

16

Survival of the Fittest

We've been taught that all life evolved from a single cell that learnt to duplicate itself. That yours and mine and that earthworm's ancestor was a single cell. How is it even possible that one evolved legs for walking and the other a squiggly shape that can burrow through soil? How come we don't see any signs of this sort of evolution happening in species now? And how did this idea come up in the first place?

It turns out that islands are really good places to watch evolution in action. This is because islands are isolated ecosystems without much interference from outside. The various species that live there adapt to the specific conditions of that island and are usually not found in other places – not even on the mainland that the island is close to. That itself tells you a lot about evolution for adaptation to a particular environment. And that is what Charles Darwin saw when the ship he was travelling in made a stop at the Galapagos Islands, off the coast of Ecuador in South America.

The Galapagos Islands are a group of many little islands in the Pacific Ocean. Each tiny island has its own ecosystem that is slightly different from the other islands, as also from the mainland. As a result, the life on each island is also slightly different from that anywhere else. Giant tortoises, marine iguanas, Galapagos penguins, the blue-footed booby and Galapagos sea lions are some of the creatures unique to these islands, but what caught Darwin's eye was the sheer variety of finches that he saw there.

He spotted at least 14 types of finches on the islands, and all of them were similar to the finch found on the mainland. This made him think that the mainland finches probably colonized the islands at some point and multiplied. However, they were all different in some way from the mainland finch.

On one island teeming with insects, Darwin saw finches with slender, pointy beaks, best suited to pry out insects from crevices in trees. On another island where the main sources of food were nuts and seeds, the finches had developed strong, thick beaks to crack open shells. Finches on an island with plenty of cactus seeds had similar thick beaks, but larger. Darwin also observed variations in the claws of the finches. Birds that spent a lot of time on the ground looking for insects had broader, flatter claws suitable for walking. Birds that spent more time perched on branches had longer hind toes, good for grasping a branch. There were noticeable differences in the overall sizes of the birds too, depending on the type and quantity of food found in their habitat.

Darwin's observation of these finches in relation to the ecosystem of their region led to a much larger idea – that as species migrated, or as the conditions of a place changed, those creatures that had a particular characteristic (such as a beak slightly longer than others) had better chances of living till they had offspring, and those without this advantageous trait perished. Generations thereafter were born with that same characteristic inherited from their parents. And they proliferated in the region where their particular trait helped them. That is how we have a whole set of finches with longer beaks and another whole set with thicker beaks.

Some of the species of finch that were observed by Charles Darwin

If you apply this idea to different species, you can see how Darwin came up with his idea of evolution, specifically that humans evolved from apes.

A this point, you are probably thinking of the chart showing human evolution that you see everywhere – the one that shows a hunched ape slowly straighten out to 'become' human. That chart is deliberately not shown in this book because it can lead to a flawed understanding of the process for so many reasons. For example, you might think, 'So if humans evolved from chimpanzees, why are chimpanzees still here? Is evolution still happening? Given enough time, will all chimps eventually take that enlightened path towards becoming human?'

Well, guess what. Evolution doesn't work like that. Chimpanzees are still around because they evolved from an extinct species to become chimpanzees. They adapted to their surroundings so well that they survived. We are their cousins, descended from another line via a common ancestor. That ancestor is extinct. Chimpanzees don't have to become us because they are so good at being themselves! If a human were to be left alone in the jungle with nothing but their birthday suit, what are their chances of survival? A lot less than a chimp, that's for sure. So which is the more evolved species in this case?

'In this case' – that's the important thing. Every species that is alive today is alive because it is at the pinnacle of its evolutionary line for the environment it is native to. Humans are alive today because they are very good at altering the environment to suit them. We can survive in deserts because we've built air-conditioned buildings, laid pipes to supply water and invented cars to move around in.

We can survive in space because we have simulated earth-like conditions in space stations. We've altered the course of rivers, flattened forests, bored through mountains, selectively bred crops and tamed animals – we've even created clones of them!

However, considering that we humans have been in existence for the time equivalent of the blink of an eye since life began on this planet, we've done all this with absolutely no idea of what our actions could lead to. Left to itself, nature takes millions of years to change. We've changed the face of the earth in a matter of a few thousand years. We could go extinct just as quickly as we arrived and the universe wouldn't even notice.

Natural Winter Clothes

Did you know that goosebumps are an evolutionary trait that helped your ancestors survive? When our ancestors had long hair that covered most of their bodies, cold weather would cause the hair follicles to contract, making the hair stand on end. In other words, they got goosebumps. This created a layer of warmth around the skin, helping people survive the cold in winter.

17

Let's Go Exploring

When Darwin set out on the *HMS Beagle* from England to South America, he put his life in the hands of the ship's captain. Luckily for him, they were very capable hands.

It was the year 1831, and navigation was a skill that required expertise in areas as diverse as geology, meteorology, biology, astronomy, mathematics and cartography, and, for the most part, even before these sciences were formally invented. It also required a high degree of physical fitness.

They didn't have many tools. Other than a compass (a device that tells you which way is north) and a sextant (a device that can help you figure out your latitude), the only other sophisticated gadget they used was a telescope.

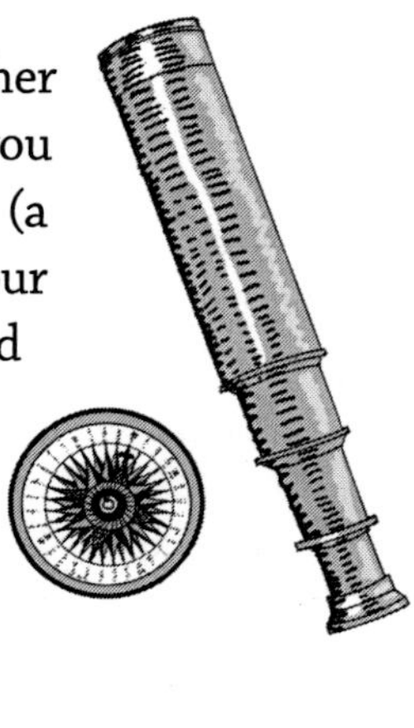

But people had made long sea journeys even before these instruments were invented. We are talking about a time almost 2,000 years before them, a time when compasses and sextants did not exist but exceptional navigational skills certainly did.

A tribe of seafarers they were, the inhabitants of the Polynesian islands in the Pacific Ocean. How else did they get there? These are some of the most remote islands on earth, some 2,000 miles away from the shore of the mainland. They saw the world as more ocean than land. Generations of Polynesians befriended the ocean and the sky. They studied the tides, the clouds, the swells, the stars, the winds and the birds until they made a near-perfect science out of the art of navigation. They were able to gauge the rhythms and patterns of nature and could navigate the thousands of miles that separated each island.

The rising and the setting of the sun and the stars told them the direction they were headed in. This, combined with the movement of ocean swells, told them the direction towards which land lay. Ocean swells are regular, stable movements of the ocean after storms have passed and the wind has died. The trade winds of the Pacific generate swells in particular directions that a skilful navigator can read.

One master navigator, Mau Piailug, in a bid to revive the lost art of his ancestors' wayfinding skills, crossed a 2,500-mile stretch of the Pacific Ocean in 1976. He set out from Hawaii without any navigational instruments. He had learnt the art of listening to the sky and the sea and the birds from his grandfather. As a child, he would play in the tide pools in different parts of the island or just sit on the beach feeling the wind, and he came to understand what subtle shifts in wind and water movements meant. He learnt traditional chants that helped him remember the many rules of navigation.

His grandfather would take him on fishing trips into the ocean on a canoe. It was then that he learnt to feel the movement of water and tell the difference between a deep, permanent current and a small one caused by the wind. He learnt to read the swells in the ocean, and based on how the swells were moving the canoe, he could tell if they were headed towards or away from land.

He could tell this because an island reflects and refracts swells. The reflection happens as the waves hit a barrier and change direction; the refraction happens as the waves move from deep to shallow waters and slow down. The waves interfere with each other and change pattern. A keen navigator can spot these changes in pattern and locate the remotest of islands.

Birds can help confirm these findings. Clusters of birds and isolated clouds on the horizon also indicate the presence of land. There are certain birds that feed on aquatic life and build their nests on land. If you identify such a bird, all you have to do is follow its flight and you will reach land.

When you are in a small canoe out in the ocean, it is important to be able to predict the weather. Mau learnt many tricks of weather forecasting by reading the clouds and the wind. If the clouds overhead are moving in the same direction as surface winds, the weather is likely to remain unchanged. But if they are moving in a different direction, then there is a chance that the surface winds may change direction.

It was a 31-day journey from Hawaii to Tahiti. With a deep and intimate understanding of nature, Mau used the knowledge of his ancestors to guide the canoe safely to land. More than 3,000 years ago, the Polynesians had perfected these same techniques to colonize tiny specks of land scattered in the vast Pacific, each thousands of miles apart from each other!

Voyages and Potatoes

A couple of thousand years after the Polynesians, in 1497, Vasco da Gama undertook a perilous journey from Lisbon to Kozhikode, sailing around the Cape of Good Hope. He had set out with a crew of 170 men, and after spending 300 days at sea, only 54 returned home with him. The rest had died of various illnesses, most commonly scurvy, a fatal disease caused by a lack of vitamin C.

The sailors had to survive on stored food for long periods of time. Vitamin C is found in fresh citrus fruits, which are perishable. So while the early European explorers were hailed for their achievements in undertaking long voyages to locate new lands for trade and conquest, it was difficult to put together a crew knowing that most of them would die before completing the journey.

One journey, however, was remarkable for the fact that there were fewer deaths from scurvy. This was because they had been eating a strange new tuber from South America that the sailors had brought into the ship as they were leaving. It was the potato, a plant unknown to the Europeans, as it is not native to that region.

Potatoes happen to be a rich source of vitamin C. They also have a longer shelf life compared to citrus fruits and can be made to last for months if stored in vinegar. In fact, the Incas had devised a method of dehydrating and mashing potatoes that would make them last 10 years!

So with potatoes on board, it was now possible to undertake longer voyages and even promise the crew that they would return home.

18

Making Maps

Now that we have sailed the open seas and learnt to navigate, here's a great idea – why not note down the routes we charted so that it's easier to visit those places a second time?

The early navigators did this; they would always put down their routes on paper and mark all the landmarks.

It's called cartography – the art of visualizing your surroundings and putting it down on paper in a way that others can comprehend. In other words, it's all about making maps.

When you look at maps of countries, aren't you struck by the minute squiggles along the borders of cities and coastlines? These maps were made long before an aerial view was available. So how did they know that the line at the coast curves in just so, and the squiggly line of a border smooths out after a while?

How did they draw maps of entire countries and coastlines stretching for hundreds of kilometres without having the ability to fly up and look at it?

Let's figure it out.

You can start by mapping out your immediate surroundings. Are you at home? What is outside your home? A road stretching out on both sides, oriented north-south perhaps? Maybe the northward road leads to a school, and the southward route leads to a mall? There's a park right opposite the house. It has a gate on the east, exiting into a road that leads to a hospital. But if you turn right soon after exiting the park, and take another right down the road, you will reach the entrance of the mall. If, however, you decide to walk on straight, you will reach the railway station.

Is this too complicated to picture in your head? Well, we can do better, let's draw a picture of it!

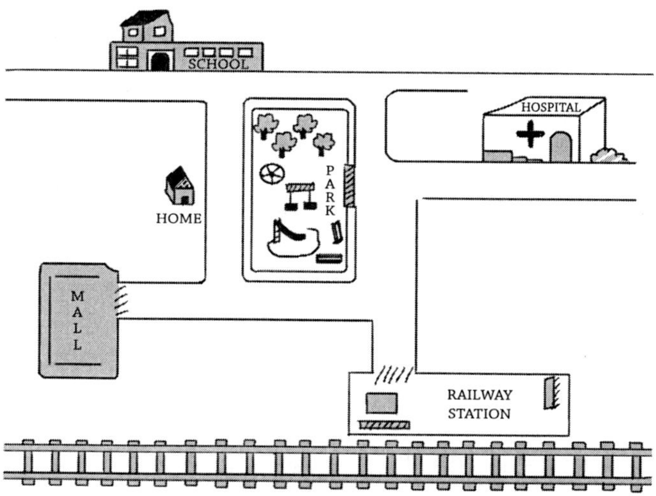

With this map, it is possible to navigate to different places within the city if you know where you are.

Now let's see a bigger map with many cities.

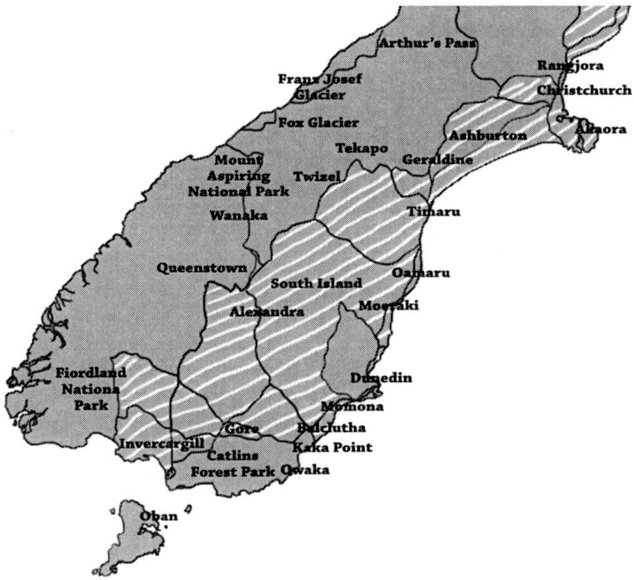

And here are the squiggly borders! How are they done?

The secret lies in triangles.

Go back to the map of the city, and put your finger on the railway station. From there, run your finger to the hospital in a straight line. Imagine that this is one side of a triangle. Let's call it the base. To complete the triangle, run your finger up to the school. That's the apex.

Now imagine that you are standing in front of the railway station. And imagine that you have measured the exact distance between the railway station and the hospital. Now, using a compass, you can measure the angles made by the other two sides of the triangle with this base line. (This is possible only if you can see the school from where you're standing.)

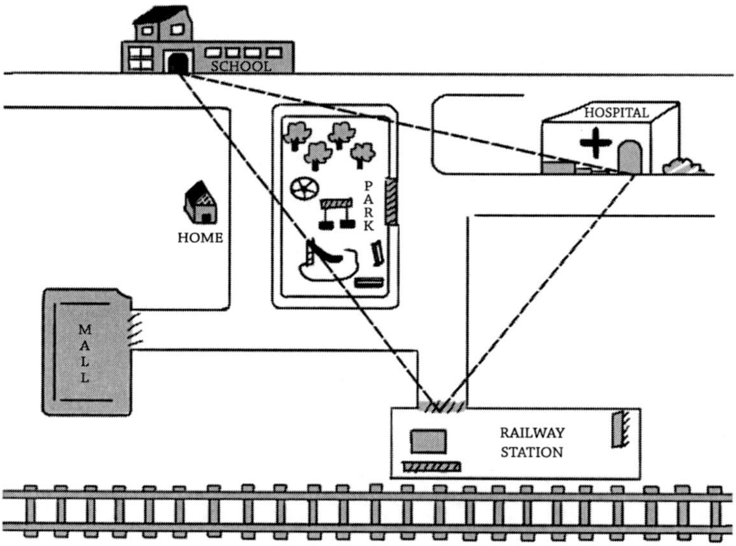

There are laws governing the construction of triangles. If you know them, good for you, but if you don't, then don't worry – it's enough to understand that some clever maths involving the length of the base and the angles made by the other two sides can give you the distance between the apex of the the triangle and the other two points. That is, you will know how far the school is from the railway station as well as the hospital, without actually having to measure the distance by foot.

Now, make another triangle with the same base but a different apex. Let's see, shall we choose the mall? Okay, so trace another triangle with your finger, like this:

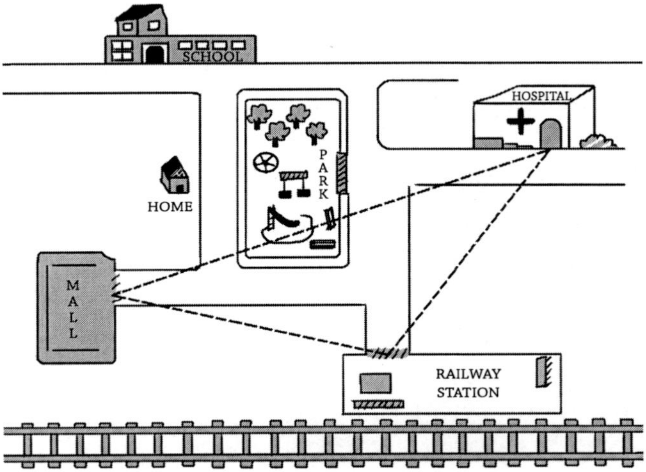

If you join the two apex points, you get a line, which could be the border joining the school and the mall! Now imagine hundreds of little triangles all drawn along the border of a city and you have your squiggly, wiggly border.

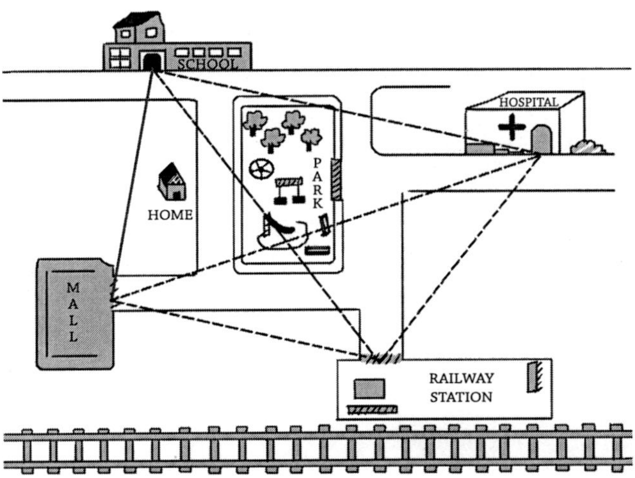

(Just so you know - There's another way of doing this: if you measure all three sides of the triangle, the angles can be calculated, and you can then use these angles to tell the direction.)

This method of surveying the land and making a chain of triangles to plot borders is known as triangulation. It was first described by a Dutch cartographer, Gemma Frisius. The first country to be accurately mapped using this method was France, in 1745, by three generations of cartographers from the Cassini family. The work was started by Giovanni Dominico Cassini, using Gemma Frisius's methods of surveying and drawing triangles. It was continued by his son Jacques Cassini and completed by his grandson César-François Cassini de Thury. It took them close to 100 years and 180 separate map sheets to produce the first scientifically drawn map of a country.

Another major triangulation effort was made by the British in India during the 18th century, with the ambitious Great Trigonometrical Survey. The entire country was mapped and measured with scientific precision for the first time, creating the contours of the peninsula with astonishing accuracy.

Today, we have satellite imagery and drones with cameras to confirm these contours, but the mathematicians from back in the day, of course, always knew they were right!

The Pundit

British engineers undertook the Great Trigonometric Survey of India in the 1850s and accurately mapped most of India. However, one part eluded them – the plateau of Tibet, known as 'the roof of the world'. Guarded by Chinese troops, this area was off limits to Europeans. But the vast uncharted territory was also coveted by the British because of its important trading centres, such as Lhasa. The Russians, too, had their eye on the same territory. The British had to empower themselves with some knowledge of the terrain if they had to defend the empire against invasions from the north. Many European surveyors were killed when they ventured out to these areas. The British had almost given up, when Captain Thomas G. Montgomerie came up with a brilliant plan to train the hill dwellers of Dehradun, Kumaon and other border areas in the art and science of clandestine surveying.

The first among them was Nain Singh, aka the Pundit.

Nain Singh underwent several rounds of training before he ventured into Tibet. First, he had to train his legs to walk at a measured pace. An *exact* measured pace – 33 inches to the stride, to be precise. So he tied a 33-inch length of cord around his ankles and practised walking for weeks and weeks, until he mastered walking with a 33-inch stride even without the cord.

Then he was trained to use surveying instruments such as a sextant (to find the latitude), a compass (to know the direction) and a thermometer (to measure the temperature).

Then his disguise was put together.

A Buddhist monk seemed best. The long flowing robes were useful for concealing his instruments. A rosary was specially made, containing exactly 100 beads, all of the same size, except for a single one that was larger than the others. He would use this to keep track of the number of paces walked, slipping one bead through his fingers for every 100 steps. On completing a full circle on the rosary, he would have taken 10,000 steps.

He would need mercury to set an artificial horizon (when the actual horizon is obscured by fog or darkness) in order to calculate the altitude. Cowrie shells sealed with wax were used to hold the mercury, which could then be poured into a monk's begging bowl when required.

But best of all was the prayer wheel. A Buddhist prayer wheel is a hollow cylinder that can be opened. Prayers written on strips of paper are put inside. The cylinder is then spun while chanting, 'Om mani padme hum,' which is believed to send the prayers straight to heaven.

Nain Singh may have found the prayers useful, as his work was extremely dangerous, but he put the prayer wheel to a more practical use.

He noted down the time, steps taken, latitude, temperature and altitude at regular intervals on strips of paper and concealed them in the prayer wheel.

He was out by himself, surveying in the toughest conditions imaginable, not just because of the high altitude and cold weather, but also because he was in constant danger of being killed as a spy if discovered with anything suspiciously un-monk-like.

At the end of his career, Nain Singh had walked more than 1,600 miles, or close to 3,160,000 steps – every single one measured, counted and noted.

19

Numbers Don't Lie

Mathematics has a way of always being right. You saw it with the triangulation in the last chapter, and now you will see it becoming the foundation on which imposing ancient structures were built.

Was it religion, or a need to touch the sky, or to be remembered for eternity – what was it that drove ancient people to build monumental structures that are still awe-inspiring and breathtaking in beauty? Whatever it was, it could not have been done without advanced mathematics. Of course, some choose to believe that aliens did it, but until we actually come in contact with any aliens, we will choose to believe that these stupendous ideas originated right here on earth.

The oldest textbook on geometry ever found is a collection of instructions for precise measurements and construction called the *Sulba Sutras*.

It's now called the Pythagorean theorem, but the *Sulba Sutras*, written some four centuries before the time of Pythagoras, mention the property of right-angled triangles (that the square of the hypotenuse is equal to the sum of the squares of the other two sides).

The *Sulba Sutras* read like a textbook of geometric principles. Using only strings and pegs, detailed procedures for creating precise geometric shapes are explained (most of the world knows this as Euclidean geometry). *Sulba* means 'string' or 'cord' and sutra means 'rule' or 'procedure', so the title translates to 'Rules of the Cord'.

These geometric shapes were not created on paper using protractor and scale, but on the ground, using strings, cords, pegs and bricks. A specific length of string was used to measure out distances and precisely constructed bricks were placed along the measured length. Following the methods described in the sutras, you could start by creating simple shapes like squares and rectangles, and then move on to more complex shapes. The sutras even tell us how to transform a square into a trapezium, triangle, rhombus and circle. What is more, this is an 'area-preserving transformation', that is, the area of the new shape is the same as that of the original square!

The reasons behind such constructions were usually ritualistic in nature. Typically, bricks were arranged in a specific formation and used as an altar for a havan. One such formation described in the sutras is the Svena-chita, or Falcon. *Five layers of bricks go into constructing this 50-foot-long falcon. Each layer needs 200 bricks of a precise size and shape. No brick should rest on another of the same shape and size.* With five layers of bricks, this altar would probably be knee-high.

These constructions are usually specified for one particular size. However, the sutras contain some handy tricks if you want to double or halve the size of the altar. You could call them theorems. Essentially, they are a set of mathematical rules, which can be used with different sets of dimensions to get different-sized structures, all with the same underlying construction principles.

So, starting with the instructions for constructing a knee-high falcon altar and applying the theorem for tripling its area, you could construct a small temple! Or a really large one, if you just use a bigger number.

Temple Tales

Angkor Wat is the largest temple in the world. Built in Cambodia during the early 12th century, it occupies 200 acres of land and its highest tower is 70 feet tall!

Inca temples were built with huge stones that perfectly interlock with each other – like a jigsaw puzzle. Researchers have replicated the blocks and come up with some astounding findings – the shape of the blocks and their centre of gravity make it possible for a single human to move the large heavy blocks without the help of machines!

The Megalithic Temples of Malta, dating back to 3500 BCE, are considered the oldest free-standing structures in the world.

The Great Pyramid of Khufu at Giza stands more than 480 feet tall. It has 2.3 million stone blocks, each weighing between 2.5 and 15 tons!

Easter Island, a tiny speck of an island in the Pacific Ocean, has a row of close to a thousand monolithic statues dotting the coastline. Carved between the 13th and 16th centuries, they are imposing structures, the tallest of them being 33 feet high and weighing 82 tons.

20

Tick-Tock

In the third century BCE, in the city of Lothal in the Indus Valley, a mother called out to her children playing outside to come home before dark. She looked at the horizon and thought that they would perhaps be able to play one more game of marbles before the sun set. It was getting colder these days, and that meant that it would get dark sooner.

A few thousand kilometres west, in ancient Egypt, another mother would do the same after some time. It was still bright there, and the sun was not as low as it was in Lothal.

A few thousand years forward, in the same place at around the same time of day, yet another mother was calling out similarly to her children. She also used the phrase 'before dark'. She didn't give them an absolute time value, such as 6 p.m. or 7.30 p.m., knowing that some winter days would see the sun set as early as 5 p.m., and she definitely did not want the children out for an hour in the dark. So a relative time, 'before dark', worked well.

'After sunrise' was another good time to schedule things, as was 'when the sun is directly overhead'.

It is no surprise then that the first timekeeping device was a sundial.

Someone noticed one sunny day that a vertical stick placed on the ground casts a shadow, and that as the day progresses, this shadow revolves around the base. So they drew a circle around the base. And they marked divisions on the circle, slicing it up into equal parts. They called it a dial. And they called the part that casts a shadow the gnomon (pronounced no-mon).

Since the sun moves from east to west, a sundial works best when the gnomon is oriented north–south.

They also started using a slanted gnomon, rather than a vertical one, and pointed it to the north pole of the sky. (If the sundial is in the southern hemisphere, it should point to the south pole of the sky.)

In the period between the years 1724 and 1734, a truly international collaboration of mathematicians resulted in the construction of the Jantar Mantar observatories in Delhi and Jaipur. The architect was Maharaja Sawai Jai Singh, who, in addition to being a Rajput emperor, was a trained mathematician and astronomer, well versed in traditional Indian methods of precise geometric construction.

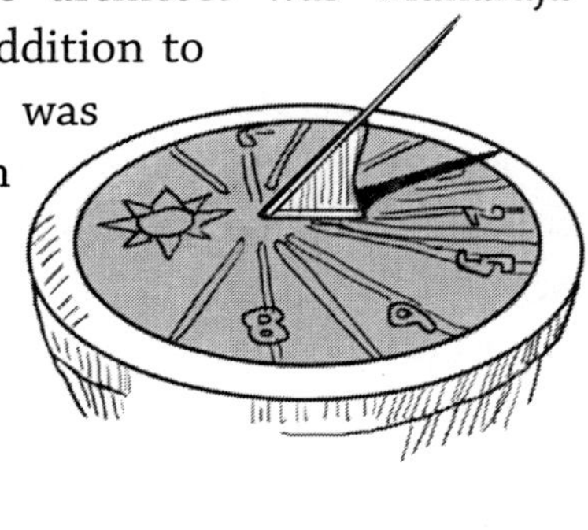

Like a good scientist, he did his research before plunging into his ambitious plan.

What was his ambitious plan?

Simply to build the largest sundial in the world.

And what was his research?

To begin with, he studied mathematical and astronomical works of the ancients – the Babylonians, the Egyptians, the Greeks, the Chinese and, of course, his own ancestors in India. He spoke to Islamic astronomers and studied their calendars. He found out about the latest developments in Greek astronomy from European travellers.

Jantar Mantar in Jaipur has a structure called the Samrat Yantra, which is one of the largest sundials in the world. At 73 feet, its gnomon is as tall as a seven-storey building. As the day progresses, the gnomon's shadow moves along the scale. There are two arc-shaped ramps on either side that reach up to 45 feet. You can climb up these ramps to watch the shadow of the gnomon fall on the scale below. The smallest division of the scale corresponds to two seconds. This means that you can read the time off this dial with an accuracy of two seconds. Before this mammoth structure was built, astronomers had small brass instruments that could not be calibrated to such precision. Sawai Jai Singh simply increased the size of his instruments by more than a hundred times and achieved a degree of accuracy never before possible.

Candle Clocks

With a sundial, you would be able to tell the time as long as there's sunlight, but what about when there isn't?

Someone came up with the clever idea of using candles.

To use a candle as a clock, you need a set of candles that are exactly alike in length, thickness, wax type, wick type and are all made in the same way. You start with two candles and a sundial.

Stand the candles next to each other, but light only one. Observe the sundial. After an hour has passed, compare the height of the burning candle with the unlit one and make a mark on the unlit one. Wait another hour, and compare the two candles again. Make another mark on the unlit candle. Do this until the first candle burns out. The unlit candle now has a series of marks running along its length. This acts as a ruler for the other candles.

So anytime during the night or when you are indoors, you can simply burn a candle, set it next to the 'ruler' and count the hours that have passed!

People then came up a bunch of ideas, not just to tell the time of the day but also to keep track of minutes, hours and days past.

Water Clocks

The water clock operates on a similar principle. Two clear tubes are required. Only one is filled with water and allowed to drip at a slow, steady rate. The other tube is used to mark the hours while observing another timepiece, such as a sundial. Once the 'ruler' is made, just like the candle clock, the water tube is set next to the ruler, and the time can be kept track of.

Hour Glass

An hour glass has become a symbol of timekeeping, possibly due to its elegance and the fact that once it is made, there is no further maintenance required. No new candles to make, no water to fill. Once the sand has fallen through, all you have to do is turn it upside down!

Mechanical clocks

The truly great breakthrough came with the invention of the mechanical clock. It didn't just keep track of the hours gone by, it also told you the exact time. And it did so without being dependent on the sun.

You have read earlier in this book (Chapter 12: To the Stars) how the ancient navigators figured how far east or west they had travelled by keeping track of the time of rise of a star in the night sky. And did you wonder how they did it before the invention of mechanical clocks? It was challenging. Essentially, they took the risk of getting hopelessly lost at sea if they did not have a reliable timepiece.

The first mechanical clock (probably made in 14th century Europe) used the principle of 'verge escapement', which means that there is a small cog (a wheel with teeth) that is attached by a stick (called the verge) to another wheel (on top of which you can place a dial). The verge is made to rotate by winding up a spring. As it rotates, the teeth of the cog catch the verge at little grooves cut in its side. This causes it to go 'tick-tock, tick-tock'.

This is an incredibly clever and delicate piece of work. As long as the timepiece was wound regularly, it kept accurate time. But did it solve the problem of seafarers?

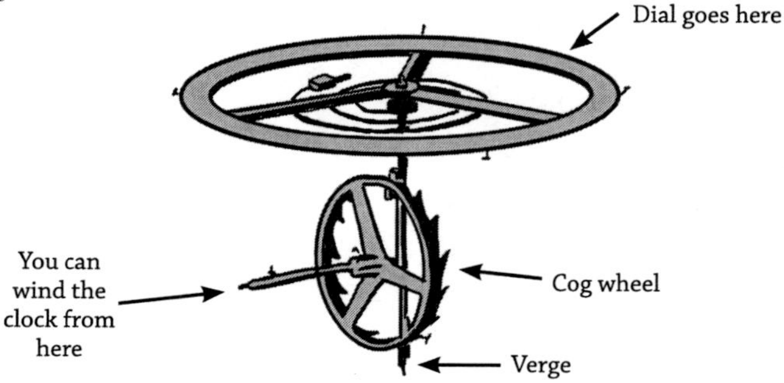

Not yet. Because on board a ship, the motion of the sea, and the variation in humidity, and other factors caused the mechanism to go awry.

Over time, a series of improvements were made, most notably the pendulum clock (designed by Galileo in the 16th century, improved on and built by Christian Huygens in the 17th century), which was highly accurate, erring by less than a minute per day. At sea, however, it was a different story. In 1707, four warships of the British navy ran aground off the coast of Sicily due to navigational errors. Close to 4,000 sailors died. The British government announced a prize of 20,000 pounds to anyone who could build an accurate sea watch. The challenge was taken up by a carpenter called John Harrison. He used ball bearings to reduce friction, two different metals to accommodate changes in temperature and humidity, and weighted balances to take care of the ship's rolling and pitching on sea. It worked, and he claimed the prize.

The real prize, however, went to European voyagers, who, powered by their accurate timepieces (and potatoes, remember Chapter 17?), reached the ends of the world, claiming, conquering and colonizing the 'new' lands.

21

Countdown to Zero

Numbers are definitely a human idea. Unlike fire, which people saw happen naturally and learnt to harvest, or weaving, which they observed being done by birds, or architecture, which they saw ants and beavers excel at, numbers and counting and mathematics are a result of the human need to organize, build and stretch the limits of what we believe is possible.

And because counting is a human idea, it was propelled by unique human needs in different parts of the world. Mesopotamia, for instance, being a trade hub for the ancient civilizations of Turkey, Babylon, Egypt and perhaps even the Indus Valley, needed to keep track of goods traded and money exchanged. Remember the story of the clay tokens? Well, the ancients had these clay tokens inside clay tablets, and they would count the tokens. Some cultures in Central Africa developed a system of tally marks to keep track of the phases of the moon. The Mayans, being brilliant astronomers, recorded precise celestial data and developed advanced calendars. The Egyptians were ambitious builders, who, with their particular fondness for pyramids, worked out geometric concepts of areas and volumes. The Romans, with their single-minded ambition of world domination, stuck to basic arithmetic, which was all their cumbersome notation would allow them.

The Indians experimented with numbers simply because they wanted to play with them some more. With their eye on the sky, they needed a perception of the vastness above, a concept as intangible as the cosmos, as abstract as the universe and as deep as philosophy. And they came up with a way of representing... nothing! It was the astronomer and mathematician Brahmagupta who first defined zero as what you get when you subtract a number from itself and used a mathematical symbol for it. You can find all this in his book *Brahmasphutasiddhanta* written in the 7th century, along with entire chapters dedicated to algebra and geometry. Brahmagupta was also the first to explain the idea of negative numbers. He called them 'debt', as opposed to 'property' which is positive.

Later mathematicians of India built upon the idea of zero and played around some more. Algebraic problems were devised in poetic, whimsical form. An ancient Jain text written on birchbark talks about the time it would take to build a yojana-high (one yojana is around 12 kilometres) cube of lamb's wool if you were to lay one strand of wool every century. And another problem asked you to find the distance travelled by a deity flying at a certain speed for six months. Clearly the ancient Indians thought in very big numbers.

It wasn't just for expressing big numbers that the zero came in handy. It really changed the way humans thought about numbers.

Take Roman numerals for instance. The notation follows a system of using one line for the number one, two lines for the number two, three lines for the number three, then comes a change in symbol for five, with four adopting that and a line to the left indicating subtraction. Six, seven and eight again have lines to the right of the symbol for five, with a change in symbol for ten and nine following the subtraction rule.

Roman Numerals

1 = I	10 = X	100 = C	1000 = M
2 = II	20 = XX	200 = CC	2000 = MM
3 = III	30 = XXX	300 = CCC	3000 MMM
4 = IV	40 = XL	400 = CD	
5 = V	50 = L	500 = D	
6 = VI	60 = LX	600 = DC	
7 = VII	70 = LXX	700 = DCC	
8 = VIII	80 = LXXX	800 = DCCC	
9 = IX	90 = XC	900 = CM	

With this set of symbols, you're good to go up to 39. Then comes a new symbol for 50, which is used to write 40 (as 10 less than 50). With this, you can go up to 89. Then you need another symbol for 100, using which you can write 90 (as 10 less than 100). This is good to take you till 399. Then you need a new symbol for 500, using which you will write 400 (as 100 less than 500). And so on.

With the introduction of zero, you need a different symbol for every number from one to nine. And then, of course, there's zero, using which you can write any number, from very large to very small. But that was not the big difference the zero made. The big idea with zero was a 'place' for every number that was associated with a 'value'. So a five in the 'tens' place has a value of 50, whereas the same five in the 'units' place is simply five.

The really radical thing about this system is that you now think of a number as an abstract entity, not used just for counting and measuring but also to create theoretical worlds with negative numbers, or the idea of negative numbers, of square roots of negative numbers, imaginary numbers, simulation, programming, the concept of a black hole, of time travel, of relativity, of the infinite and of the infinitesimal...

22

The Right Remedies

Third century BCE, somewhere along the banks of the Chenab River in Punjab

They had been waiting outside her dwelling for three days. She would not come out despite earnest requests. But that was expected. They were not surprised, just deeply disappointed. But they did not give up. They had heard that it sometimes took her weeks to emerge. It was said that she would just sit with her eyes closed and the sufferer's ailments would become known to her through some divine mechanism. If you were desperate enough, you stayed until she appeared, or until the patient died.

This particular patient was holding on. Sinking, but holding on. He was young, still a boy, lying on his back on a sack on the ground. His mother cradled his head on her lap. 'My boy is burning!' she wailed.

'The boy is burning,' said a small child who was looking out of the doctor's dwelling through a chink in the wall.

'Hmmmm,' said his grandmother. She chose a few herbs and powders from a shelf and put them into a small stone mortar. Picking up the pestle, she began to grind them together while simultaneously instructing her grandson, 'Charu, wet that piece of cloth and take it to them. Ask them to place it on the boy's forehead to cool him down.'

Charu had already soaked the cloth and was wringing the water out. He knew what to do. He had been his grandmother's apprentice for years.

The patient's relatives had been eagerly waiting for the famed healer to open the door and were slightly disappointed to see a little boy instead. Still, he was better than nothing. They accepted the damp cloth and followed his instructions.

After a while, the old lady emerged with the mortar. She gave it to her apprentice and started examining the patient while asking questions. Thumb on pulse, she asked how long his body had been burning. Hand gently pressing his stomach, she wanted to know the details of his bowel movements, about body aches, if any, about chills, coughs and whether the boy had eaten anything.

Her grandson listened to every question and answer attentively, memorizing everything, as he had done for the last three years. At the same time, he ground the herbs in the mortar to a fine paste.

The healer gave the paste to the boy's mother. 'Give your son this medicine three times a day for three days. This is to make sure his body cools down. If he is able to eat, give him some mashed rice.'

The healer's grandson added, 'Store the medicine in a cool, dry place.'

This boy may be a figment of my imagination, or he may have existed. He may even have gone on to compose the 8,500 verses found in the *Charaka Samhita*, a defining work of Ayurveda written in ancient India sometime between the second and fourth century BCE. The text is in Sanskrit, and the style is poetry. Medical science explained in verse. Why verse? To make it easy to recall. Remember, this was before printing technology was known. If you wanted to make copies of books, you had to write every word down or hire scribes to do so. It was common practice to memorize theory, and words in rhythm and metre are easier to learn by heart.

The *Charaka Samhita* is the foundation of Ayurveda. It explains, among other things, the working of the human body in terms of three doshas or properties: vata (air/gas), pitta (fire) and kapha (phlegm/moisture). When they are in balance, a person is healthy, but if one of them is in excess or in dearth, the person will experience disease or disorder until balance is restored.

Meanwhile, some 5,000 kilometres away, on the island of Kos in ancient Greece, the *Hippocratic Corpus* was being composed. Perhaps written by Hippocrates himself, or by his apprentices, it is a collection of 60 medical works, including the Hippocratic oath, which doctors to this day swear upon. Interestingly, these works also talk about 'humours' or vital body fluids: blood, bile and phlegm. Although the details differ from Ayurveda, both approaches associate the imbalance of these humours with illnesses.

The ancient Mayans also believed in maintaining balance between the opposing forces of hot and cold. Foods such as garlic, pepper and ginger were considered hot, whereas cheese and milk were cold. Illnesses such as fever, diarrhoea and vomiting were classified as hot, whereas paralysis and constipation were cold. They believed in treating a hot illness with cold food and a cold illness with hot food. However, they also believed that eating hot and cold foods together caused shock to the system and resulted in disorders.

Over in China, balance had to be achieved between the forces of yin and yang so that the life force, qi, could flow unobstructed throughout the body. Any imbalance would result in illness, which was tackled by inserting fine needles at specific points in the body, in the belief that these small punctures would restore balance and cause the qi to move freely.

The Egyptians were more concerned with the afterlife, or what happened after death. They believed that a perfectly preserved body would continue to live on in the next world, and so they figured out a way to prevent the body from decomposing.

For this they had to remove all the internal organs of the body. They started with the brain. Carefully inserting a hooked surgical instrument through the nostrils, they pulled out bits of brain tissue until the entire brain was out. This was an extremely delicate operation as they had to take care to keep the face undamaged while getting every last bit of brain tissue out.

Next, they made an incision on the left side of the abdomen and carefully extracted all the internal organs. They only left the heart in place. Then they covered the body with natron, a type of salt that absorbs all moisture, leaving only a dried outer shell. This outer shell was then wrapped in strips of linen. This entire process was accompanied by ritualistic chanting.

This process of embalming was supposed to ensure a smooth passage for the soul to travel through the underworld and successfully enter the afterlife. Whether or not they succeeded at this, one thing is for sure: their preservation techniques were so good that 5,000-year-old mummies have been found in perfect condition – so perfect that you can even make out their features and get an idea of what they must have looked like all those years ago!

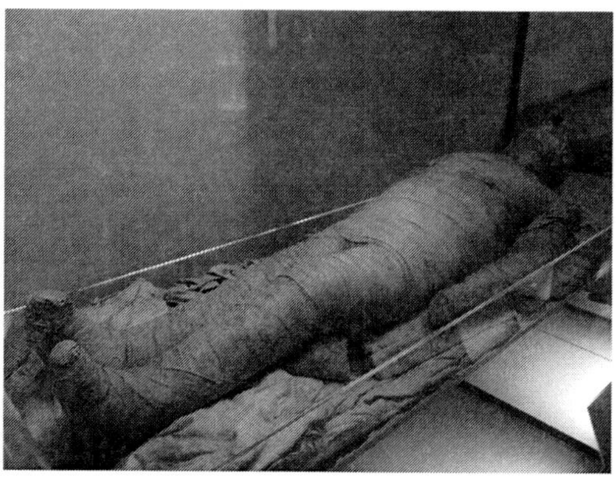

Ancient Surgery

The *Sushruta Samhita* and the *Charaka Samhita*, about which you read earlier in this chapter, are two of the oldest textbooks on medicine. While the *Charaka Samhita* focuses on internal medicine, the *Sushruta Samhita* is mostly about surgery. Before trying out surgery on humans, medical students are advised to first practise by peeling fruits and carefully extracting the seeds, and by making incisions on the skins of dead animals. A detailed procedure for performing cataract surgery is the highlight of this book. The cataract operation was considered successful if, after the procedure, the lens 'assumed the glossiness of a resplendent cloudless sun'.

The Mayans of South and Meso-America performed dental surgeries by filling cavities with semi-precious stones like jade, quartz and turquoise.

In Egypt's Saqqara lies the tomb of Merit-Ptah, who was one of the first female physicians known by name. She lived in 2700 BCE and has been described as the 'chief physician' by the hieroglyphs present on her tomb. Not much is known about her, but later writings suggest that a strong line of female physicians practised and thrived in ancient Egypt.

The Accidental Discovery of Anaesthesia

For 50 years after the discovery of laughing gas, or nitrous oxide, people used it only to amuse themselves. They held 'laughing parties', where the idea was to get together, inhale nitrous oxide and laugh uncontrollably. While in hospitals, patients would go through unimaginable pain under the surgeon's knife because anaesthesia was not yet known. One day, at a laughing party, one of the participants fell off his chair laughing, and despite a huge gash on his body from which blood gushed forth, continued to laugh. A dentist, Horace Wells, observed this and used laughing gas on his next patient for a tooth extraction, with the happy result that the patient experienced very little pain.

23

Down the Drain

When it comes to dealing with our excretory functions, we all have different ideas.

Some like to wash, some like to wipe. Some think squatting is a good idea, others prefer sitting. A bucket and mug work well for some, others want a sprayer to wash up. The wipers prefer the paper to be soft, with preferences ranging from two-ply to quilted. A few are content to flush their excreta by pouring water from a bucket, while others prefer to have a tank filled with water that flushes when a lever or button is pressed.

But flush it where?

That's where the really good ideas come in.

It turns out that more than 4,000 years ago, the people of the Indus Valley hit upon a neat solution to take care of city-wide sanitation. They had houses with attached bathrooms, and sometimes a separate latrine. The floor was laid with flat stones, sloping towards the drain leading outside. A pipe made of terracotta connected the toilet's drain to the sewer outside. This small sewer would join the larger main sewer that ran across the city. The sewers were made with smooth bricks joined together seamlessly to make them watertight and prevent leaching of the waste. The entire network of drains was laid underground, showing expertise in masonry. People would pour water to flush out their waste, making this a pretty advanced system for such an old civilization.

Some 4,700 kilometres to the west of the Indus Valley, the Minoan civilization of Greece had similar underground sewer pipes, and had cisterns filled with water for flushing, too!

The ancient Romans made defecation a social activity. A 2,000-year-old public toilet has been unearthed, which is essentially a long slab of stone with keyhole-shaped cuts at intervals. A continuous stream of water ran below the 'seats'. People would sit on these

openings and do their business while having a friendly chat with the person next to them. I told you it was a 'public' toilet!

The stream of water was part of the network of sewers running throughout the city, similar to the system in the Indus Valley.

After all this advanced engineering, for some reason, we regressed.

Later civilizations did not give much thought to sanitation, and things really started going downhill. Literally even, as people would retreat to the small hillocks behind their villages to do their business.

As things stand, the consensus is that we've not really hit upon the best idea to manage our bodily wastes. Because even if we all have beautiful bathrooms and toilets in our houses, where do you suppose all the waste goes? As the human population increases, it does not become sustainable to let it all out into rivers and hope the running water just takes it away.

Many cities have sewage treatment plants that sanitize the waste before letting it out into rivers. However, these can be set up only if there is plenty of space available, and they require a good deal of money.

How about putting the waste to use?

Waterless toilets do just that.

Here's how a waterless toilet is made: You need to make sure that you don't let the urine and the faeces mix. No, it's not as gross as it sounds – the pot just needs to be designed in a clever way. Like having a sloping bamboo mat act as a sieve that will allow the

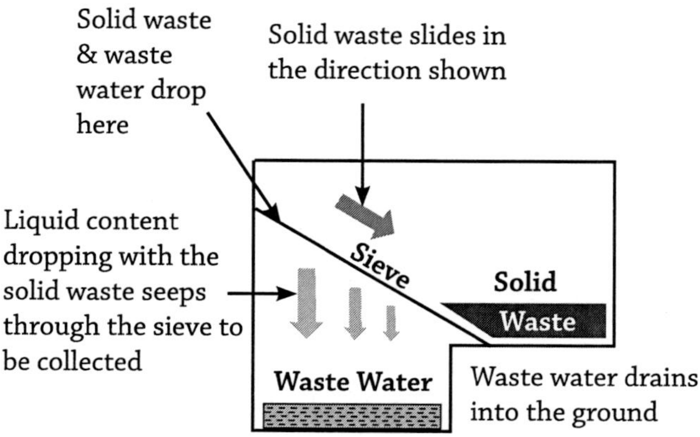

Solid Waste Collection Pit

waste water to pass through, but can hold the poop and send it to a different pit.

Since urine by itself is not harmful (it's only the bacteria that collect on open urine that cause the smell and the hazard), it can be safely let into the ground or put to use. Here's how: hydrogen can be separated from the urine and used to fuel a generator.

Urine also has nitrogen, phosphorus and potassium, which are great ingredients for fertilizers.

Now that the urine is taken care of, what do we do with the solid waste? Well, if it is properly mixed with ash and grass, and allowed to rest in a pit, millions of bacteria will break it down into perfectly useful compost for agriculture.

These toilets will help us build a world where there is no 'waste'. Instead of letting sewage pollute our lakes and rivers, we can turn it into something useful.

Now, isn't that a neat idea!

24

In Your Element

Late 17th century, Hamburg, Germany

The alchemist entered his lab with a gleam in his eye. He was thinking of gold. That beautiful yellow metal, the most majestic of them all, lustrous beyond compare, so noble, so divine. He had spent his entire life thinking about gold and how to create the noble metal from a base element. For years, he had experimented with lead and then mercury, and countless other substances, but without success.

Today was going to be different.

He looked at the walls lined with shelves containing salts, acids and all sorts of colourful reagents – some powdery, some crystalline, some liquid, some bubbling, some frothing, some placid. On the far side of the lab was a cauldron under a chimney. It was on the boil, and the air was thick with a pungent odour.

The alchemist dipped a long ladle into the cauldron and poured the stinky liquid into a glass jar. He quickly closed the lid of the jar. His face contorted as the pungent fumes from the boiling cauldron enveloped him. Emerging from the fog, he placed the jar on his workbench. Then he sat in front of it and stared. And stared. And stared.

The jar of yellow waxy matter stared back at him.

'Months and months...' he grumbled to himself. 'Months and months of boiling, mixing, filtering, skimming...' He sighed. 'Ah, Hennig.' He was addressing himself, as all mad scientists do. 'All that pee.'

What was that? Did he just say pee? As in urine?

'How I convinced that entire battalion of soldiers to pee for me, every day they were stationed here,' he continued murmuring. 'Barrels and barrels. Mixing, boiling, filtering, skimming...'

Ewww, he really did say pee!

'And not just because it was yellow, you know. There was some solid science behind my reasoning.' He paused to think. The reasoning had temporarily slipped his mind. But it had seemed like a good idea at the time.

He had begun by boiling a barrel full of urine till the water evaporated. He had continued to let it simmer till it reached a thick, syrupy consistency. Then he had put some of it in a small glass jar, closed the lid and let it sit to see if anything would happen.

But nothing did. So he heated it some more and experimented on different sets by adding various ingredients and observing the outcomes. One ingredient that gave an interesting result was sand. As he stirred in some sand, a layer of oil formed on top. He skimmed it off and continued heating the residue. After a while, it became powdery. Then he put some oil back in, just to see what would happen. It had acquired a translucent, waxy texture.

At every stage, he would scoop out a little of the concoction and store it in an airtight glass jar and let it rest, hoping it would turn into gold.

As he stared, the translucent waxy substance in one of the jars began to glow.

Oh my God. Could it be turning into gold?

He held his breath.

It was a faint greenish glow at first, and it started getting brighter as the alchemist's eyes grew wider. Excitedly, he took the lid off the case – and it spontaneously burst into flames!

It was spectacular, but it was not gold.

The alchemist sank to the floor. Did his life's work just go up in flames?

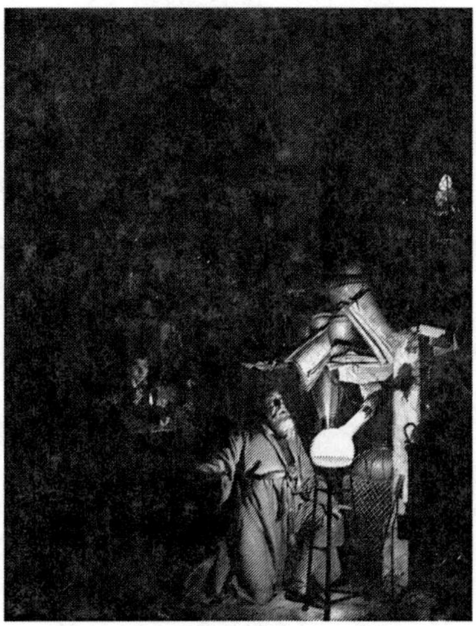

The Alchemist Discovering Phosphorus by Joseph Wright

The Element Phosphorus

What was it that Hennig Brand did?

Urine is an organic carbon-based compound containing phosphates. With all his heating and stirring, the alchemist, Hennig Brand, had managed to release elemental phosphorus from urine, thus becoming the first person to discover an element.

The account you just read is a fictionalized version of how he managed to do it.

Phosphorus spontaneously bursts into flames when exposed to air. So it was a good thing that he kept it in an airtight jar.

When this kind of phosphorus (known as white phosphorus) is heated to a temperature of 300 degrees in the absence of air, it turns into red phosphorus. Red phosphorus is stable. It does not burst into flames on contact with air. But when struck on an abrasive surface, it catches fire. This led to the invention of the matchstick.

The Iron Pillar

Phosphorus was not completely unknown before Hennig Brand's experiments. The huge Iron Pillar of Delhi, built in the fifth century CE, is known for its high resistance to corrosion. The reason for this is the presence of phosphorus in the iron. The ancient ironsmiths had perfected a process of smelting that would not wash away the phosphorus in slag (as it happens in modern furnaces).

Now, that's a much better way of using phosphorus... and it doesn't involve pee!

Alchemists

Playing with chemicals can produce unexpected results. It's almost like magic. Even something as simple as litmus turning red on contact with an acid and blue on contact with a base. When calcium gluconate pellets are heated, they expand into snake-like formations. A careful mix of bromine and acid can produce colourful patterns that are mesmerizing. When a mixture of sodium arsenite and glacial acetic acid suspended in water is added to another suspension of sodium thiosulphate in water, the clear solution turns to the colour of gold after about 30 minutes. Is it any wonder then that alchemists believed that with the right ingredients mixed in the right quantities in the right conditions, they could turn any metal into gold!

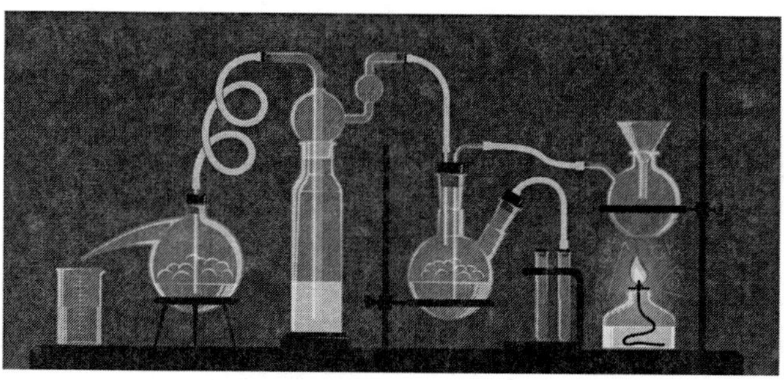

25

Game Changers

What's an idea good for? Some groundbreaking new invention that will change the course of history, perhaps? Or something so clever that we wonder how people lived without it? Or a great new insight that makes complete sense of our universe?

Maybe it's just to play games.

Playing games is serious business. Otherwise why would anyone go to all that trouble to come up with watertight rules, and why would so many people follow these rules and play with focus, giving it their all? And wouldn't it require the most inventive minds to come up with the concepts of some of the most popular games we play today, whose origins can be traced back to more than a couple of thousand years ago?

Was it a bored kid who came up with the idea of playing a game? Or a group of children who imitated their adults in pretend wars and business games? Were the best minds of the kingdom employed by a king to invent board games to help him pass the time?

The oldest board game that we have found so far is an Egyptian game called *senet*. It is more than 5,000 years old.

No one knows the rules of this game or how it was played by the ancient Egyptians. From the actual board dug up by archaeologists, we know that the grid of the game board has three rows of 10 squares each. Players sit across each other and get five pieces each to begin with. You could roll the dice to see who goes first, but why use dice when you have *senet* sticks? *Senet* sticks are oblong, with one long side painted black and the other white. They are usually four in number and tossed together. Some land with the black side up, some with the white side up. Since no official rulebook of this game exists, you can make up your own rules to interpret the *senet* sticks! You could, if you like, make a rule that says: if you have three black sides and one white, you can move one square forward. Or if your toss results in two black and two white sticks, you could decide that it means: move two squares forward and lose a turn. If you come up with all black sides, you could perhaps reward yourself with an extra turn. The possibilities are endless. And we haven't even started playing yet!

One of the oldest outdoor games to be ever played is *ōllamaliztli*, played using a rubber ball made from the famous rubber plantations of Meso-America. The non-deadly version of the game goes something like this: Two teams occupy their positions on opposite sides of a court. The court would have to be rectangular, roughly the size of a volleyball court. In fact, the game is a bit like volleyball; the two teams have to pass the ball back and forth until one team fails to return it. They are not allowed to use their limbs to hit the ball, only their hips, knees and shoulders. Sometimes, players wore leather or cloth strips over their knees and hips to protect themselves.

Well, that was the non-deadly version. What's the deadly version? Hmm... let's just say that on the losing side, heads would roll. And did I mention, the rubber

balls were 10 to 12 inches in diameter and weighed anywhere between 2 and 5 kilograms!

Some variations of this game had a sort of hoop. The ball court at the Maya temple, Chichen Itza, has a hoop made of stone.

Another Place, Another Game

Some 15,000 kilometres east of Meso-America, in a little village in south India, a group of children ran excitedly to a little clearing in the woods. This flat area surrounded by trees was their playground. Subbi had with her a nice new ball made of cloth. Her mother had saved up strips of cloth over several weeks, and when she had collected enough, she rolled them and stitched them together in the shape of a ball for her daughter to play with.

Along with Subbi were her friends Ramu, Jagga, Kittu, Ranga and Champa.

The boys and girls were planning to spend the morning playing *lagori*.

They divided themselves into two teams: Champa, Ramu and Jagga as the defenders, and Kittu, Ranga and Subbi as the attackers.

The defenders rummaged about to select seven flat stones. Once they found stones of a good size and shape, they gathered at the centre of their playing field. Ramu stacked up the stones in descending order of size. He put the biggest one at the bottom and smaller ones on top so that the column of stone was stable. The defenders then positioned themselves around the column.

Subbi prepared to launch the first attack. Standing 10 paces away from the stones, she took aim and threw the cloth ball. It was a perfect hit! The stones came down, and at the same instant the three defenders ran to build it up again. They had to be quick because the rest of the attackers had also jumped into the field. Kittu snatched up Subbi's ball and threw it at Champa. She deftly avoided it, and Ranga ran towards it.

Ranga's aim was good. Scooping up the ball, he launched it at Jagga, who was trying to build the pile back up. The ball hit Jagga's shoulder, and he had to sit out for the rest of the game. The defenders were down to two. They had to be careful. Champa and Ramu worked out a quick strategy while running to dodge the ball, now being thrown with gusto by the attackers. Champa distracted the attackers by running haphazardly, while Ramu quickly picked up the biggest stone. The attackers, sensing this strategy, aimed at Ramu, but Champa was ready with the next three stones and quickly piled them on top. Ramu was now zigzagging through the attackers. So they shifted focus to Champa again, but he raced towards the stones and piled all the remaining ones! *LAGORI*!

The first round done, the defenders and the attackers switched roles. They played a few more rounds, and, as it happens with inventive minds, the game evolved into a slightly different version. The pile of stones forgotten, the players simply pelted each other with the ball. They retained the old teams because revenge had to be had, and at the end of play there were more victories than bruises. That might not have been the case had they played with a rubber ball of the Meso-American variety!

26

A Few of Our Favourite Foods

'Can I have some *xocolatl*?'[1] asked the little Aztec boy.

His mother shushed him, but the damage was done. The high priest had heard it and was giving the boy a stern look.

The little boy hid behind his mother and stayed quiet for the rest of the ceremony.

It was a grand ceremony conducted by the high priests to ensure that their emperor, Montezuma II, had a long and healthy life. An elaborate set of rituals would be performed at the end, during which the emperor would consume a goblet of *xocolatl*, the sacred drink, the 'gift from the gods', a concoction made from the beans of the cacao tree. It was not just a general plea for health.

[1] We don't know for sure if the Aztecs used the word *xocolatl* to mean a drink made with cocoa. It certainly sounds like 'chocolate', but historians are still debating this.

The emperor was about to go to battle with the invading Spanish armies. He believed that the drink would give him extra power and energy to fight the conquering forces. Only the great emperor and his fighting soldiers were allowed to drink this precious liquid. It was not meant for mere mortals.

But the little boy had tasted it at his uncle's wedding. Ordinary folk could only have this drink at weddings and other important celebrations. But ah... once you had a sip, you would never forget the taste. And having to watch while another consumed it was sheer agony.

Quietly, he slipped away from the crowd and sneaked towards the large tents where the chief cooks were entrusted with preparing the sacred drink. Choosing a safe spot, he lay on the ground, slowly lifted up the base of the tent and peeped inside.

On one end was an assistant cook, sorting the dark brown seeds and selecting only the best ones for the royal drink. These chosen seeds were then roasted by another cook on a low flame. Once they produced the perfect aroma, the seeds were transferred to a pestle and were ground. The fine powder was then moved to a large pot. Into this, water was poured in small quantities and the mixture was stirred till a smooth paste was formed. Finally, the chief cook took some of this paste into a ceremonial cup, added some water and, with great solemnity, added the final touch – a pinch of chilli powder. An assistant brought forth an ornate tray upon which the cup was placed and taken away to the ceremonial hall to be presented to the emperor.

The little boy watched all this with his mouth open, for he loved the whole process, the smells, the sounds of roasting, grinding and mixing, and, most of all, that time when all the cooks had their backs turned to him and he slowly extended his hand inside and scooped out a handful of powdered cocoa! He skipped the chilli powder, though. He preferred his *xocolatl* with honey.

The First Humans to Consume Cocoa

The Olmecs, one of the oldest known civilizations of Meso-America, were probably the first humans to harvest the seed of the cacao tree and consume it. They liked it bitter and in liquid form. They passed on their knowledge of harvesting the plants, extracting the seeds, roasting them, fermenting them, grinding them and consuming them with different additives (like vanilla, honey, chilli powder and a dozen different flavouring substances) to their successors, the Maya and the Aztec people. These civilizations flourished between 1400 BCE and 1500 CE.

Coffee and Tea

Coffee and tea were known to many ancient civilizations. They also spread across the ancient world through travellers who were foodies. For these are pleasure foods, not necessarily required for survival or nutrition. Of these, tea is perhaps the most ancient, having been referred to in a book called *The Divine Farmer's Materia Medica*, which is the translation of a 2,000-year old Chinese work 'Shen Nong Ben Cao Jing'. It talks about not only making tea but also the procedure to buy and sell tea, making it clear that tea had already become an important trading commodity.

Coffee seems to be relatively newer. The earliest mentions of coffee, that we know of, have been made in the 11th century. Believed to have originated in Ethiopia, it caught the fancy of travellers and soon travelled to the Arabian peninsula, south India, Persia and Turkey.

Istanbul may have been where the first coffee house was established. This was way back in 1475. It was called Kiva Han, and it served only black coffee. A hundred years later, coffee houses came up in parts of Europe, where they started adding milk, cream and sugar.

No matter how the coffee was served, coffee houses across centuries and countries have always had one thing in common – they were places to socialize, have intellectual debates, hatch revolutionary plots, exchange news and have business meetings. Key meetings between Indian freedom fighters took place in coffee houses, as did those of the French Revolution. In Mecca, coffee houses were even banned for a few years as they were suspected to cause people to think radically.

Salt

When it came to causing political upheaval, salt was not far behind. Mahatma Gandhi's Salt Satyagraha was the one movement that motivated the people of India into protesting against the unjust tax on salt. Not just that, the British had even prohibited people from making their own salt. And because you can't cook without salt, this worked well for the oppressors.

Salt wars have been fought at various points in history, such as the San Elizario Salt War, in which groups fought for control over the salt lakes of West Texas in the mid-19th century. During the American Revolution, the British prevented salt from reaching the revolutionaries so that they would be unable to preserve their food.

This ability of salt to preserve food is probably what makes it so special. The ancient Egyptians figured this out quite early on. Apart from preserving meat by rubbing salt on it and storing it in ceramic jars, they also used salt to preserve mummified bodies!

Salt has also made its way into some very expressive idioms[2]...

'To rub salt into the wound' – To make a hurtful experience even more painful for someone.

'Salt the books' – To implant wrong information about a financial transaction or account.

'The salt of the earth' – A group of people or a person considered highly honest or very reliable.

'Old salt' – An old sailor, someone who specifically has a lot of experience on the seas.

...seasoning the English language, you could say.

[2] An idiom is a way of saying something without really saying it, but instead using a phrase established by long usage, whose literal meaning has nothing to do with what you are trying to say! For example, if I want to tell you that you are overreacting to something trivial, I'd say, 'Don't make a mountain out of a molehill', and if you were familiar with the phrase, you would understand my meaning although there is neither a mountain nor a molehill anywhere in sight. And if you wanted me to get straight to the point, you would say, 'Don't beat around the bush.' And I might reply, 'Fine, I'll give it to you in a nutshell...'

27

You've Got Mail

Four intrepid explorers, equipped with heavy sticks, water bottles, mosquito repellant and a burning ambition to become the first Europeans to explore west Africa, silently stepped off the beach and into the forest. Their leader poked his stick carefully through the undergrowth before stepping through. His friends followed with caution. Even intrepid explorers do not want to get bitten by venomous creatures.

There was not a soul in sight. From a distance they could hear the rhythm of steadily beating drums.

The leader of the expedition had a map with him, on which he had marked out the course of the river Ogowé. His companions trusted him to follow the map and lead them into the unknown. Explorers before him had only traced the route a few miles inland. His destination was even farther down the riverbank, to the village of the Bulu people. They were legendary for their skills in drum craft, famed for both making and playing their percussion instruments. He was sure that the drumbeats came from the Bulu village.

The leader wondered how the party would be received. The Bulu people had probably never seen white-skinned Europeans before. Their features and the colour of their skin and hair would look strange to the Bulu. Would they be hostile? Should he try to catch their attention from a safe distance and gauge their reaction, so that he would have time to flee if things turned sour? Should he give them some advance sign that his group was walking towards their village? Should they stop walking so silently and make some noise?

The sound of the drums got louder. The leader made his way forward with great caution. His companions followed noiselessly. They were proud of their ability to move with stealth and silence. 'Like panthers,' he whispered to his companions. The drumbeats changed rhythm and now seemed much closer.

Actually, they seemed to be coming from right above!

The group turned their heads upwards and were astonished to see, perched above, a man with a small drum, belting out a rhythm. Then they looked behind him and saw that there were more drummers grinning down at them. They smiled nervously back.

The Bulu men had stopped drumming and were just watching.

The explorers took a tentative step forward.

The Bulu men continued watching expressionlessly.

Three more steps, and the explorers found themselves in a clearing.

Standing in the centre of the clearing was a grand welcome committee of sorts. The village chief stood there, smiling, flanked by two assistants holding four small carved objects by way of gifts for the four explorers.

The leader was astounded. He was just beginning to realize that the drumbeats were a form of communication. The drummers had conveyed not just the fact that a group was approaching their village but also the number of people that made up the group!

Tom-tomming

The phrase 'tom-tomming', an idiomatic way of saying gossiping, has its origins in a kind of drum used by African tribes to communicate. Wooden drums called tom-toms would beat out different rhythm patterns to communicate anything from proclamations of war, wedding invitations and news of death or sickness to alerts for missing persons. They could also beat out specific messages to individuals, with even their names worked into the beats.

How did they manage this? The answer lies in the very nature of the language, which relies more on the tone of voice rather than on actual words. The drums are specially made to produce distinct tones, from high to

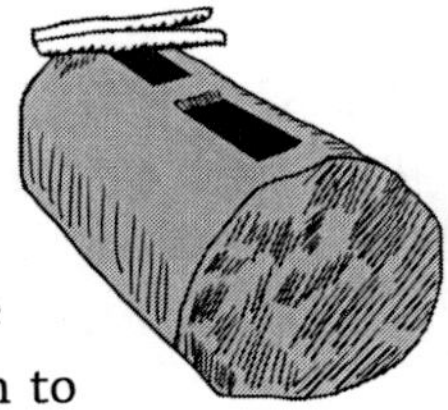

low. So what the drummer beats out is not words, but a series of tones.

A professional drum maker chooses some good hardwood (such as *lengue*, *acajou* or *iroko*) to start with. Drums can range from 2 to 4 feet in length, depending on the topography of the region and how far the sound has to carry. The log is hollowed out by making a lengthwise slit that is around 3 to 4 inches wide. The hollowing out must be a careful process, as you do not want cracks or holes in the side. After hollowing out, the thickness of the curved sides of the log should not be more than half an inch. The ends of the log would be left 3 to 4 inches thick. One end would be thicker than the other so as to produce high and low tones.

Most drums can be heard at distances of 5 to 6 kilometres away. Some are known to carry up to 20 kilometres in the absolute quiet of the night, but the different tones would not be distinguishable.

To make it easier to be understood, drum calls use a series of preset phrases (like idioms), so even if you miss hearing a couple of beats, you can always piece together the whole message from the bits you heard. For example, the phrase 'Bulu Bulu on one side, Fang Fang on the other side' would be interpreted as a call to a wrestling match. And the rather cryptic 'He only folds his hands on his breast' means that someone has died.

Homing Pigeons

Pigeons have a remarkable ability to mark out routes and follow them unerringly. They are called homing pigeons because they always find their way home. They have been known to fly hundreds of kilometres before returning safely home, and this is because they are born with something called magnetoreception. This enables the bird to detect the earth's magnetic field and orient itself. It also uses the position and angle of the sun to determine direction, and it can detect altitude and location.

But how do they know where to go?

Almost all ancient civilizations figured this out, some as far back as 5,000 years ago! Here is what we think they did, and this is what we do even today to train the pigeons.

First we make a really nice, comfortable home with plenty of stored food. This is to make sure that the pigeons *want* to return home. We start the training with birds that are six to eight weeks old. At this stage, they are familiar with their homes and are old enough to venture out alone.

To begin with, they are let out of their loft to walk about in a closed space. Then they are helped back home and fed. Over time, they learn to associate their home with food, and they always return when hungry. As they grow older, the distance they can roam about is increased, and they fly outside and return to their coop.

So the return is taken care of, but the question remains – how do they know where to go? Actually, they don't, and there is no way to tell them! Pigeons can be taken and left anywhere, but they can only fly back home.

So, say you live in Bangalore and have a friend in Bhopal who wants to send you messages. You have a set of trained pigeons who can fly to your Bangalore home. You pack your birds in a crate and go all the way to Bhopal and leave the crate with your friend. When your friend has something to say to you, she can write the message on a small piece of paper, roll it up, put it in a small glass or plastic tube (it has to be something lightweight) and fasten it to the bird's leg. Then, she can simply set the bird free, and it will fly to your home in Bangalore, which was its own home to begin with!

What if you want to reply to your friend in Bhopal? Well, she'd have to raise her own set of homing pigeons and deposit a few with you.

A really useful scenario is if you're going to travel the world and you want to send messages to your parents from different places. You would have to take a bunch of birds along with you and release them with messages, and they would reach home!

War Heroes

Pigeons were used in the World Wars when radio communication was not available or not secure enough. Soldiers carried specially constructed ventilated backpacks that could hold four to six birds. The soldiers could then send messages about their situation on the battlefield back to the base camp. The birds were particularly useful when soldiers had to ask for medical help. Many of the birds were even given medals after the war!

However, it wasn't the first time that pigeons were used in war. More than 2,000 years ago, Roman armies

used pigeons to send messages across battalions, and in a different kind of war, the winners of the ancient Olympic games were announced by pigeon post.

What if you don't have trained pigeons with you, nor drums to beat out a message? What if you are on the battlefield and you see the enemy advancing and you need to alert your forces over on the other side of the mountain?

You could do what this young Cherokee warrior did.

Small Foot was scouting an area near the border of his village. It was a regular lookout drill, on which he was sent every evening. His task was to make sure there were no suspicious activities taking place along the borders of their land. That evening, after the usual drill, he put his ear to the ground and listened very carefully. His highly sensitive ears caught the distant vibration of galloping hooves.

He had to warn his people of an approaching party. He had no idea if they were friendly or hostile, but it was always better to be prepared. Judging by the sound he had heard from the ground, they were approaching fast. He did not have enough time to run down and tell his people to be ready.

So, he quickly made a fire by striking flint and pyrite, letting the spark catch fire on some dry tinder. Once the fire got going, he added some grass and animal dung to the fire. This caused the smoke to turn thick and black.

Small Foot allowed the black smoke to rise up for a few seconds. Then, he held a blanket over the fire to prevent the smoke from rising further. He looked in the direction of the village to see if there was a response.

A minute or so later, there was an answering puff of smoke from the village.

This meant that they had seen his first smoke signal and were waiting for the message.

Small Foot then lifted the blanket and allowed a small puff of smoke to escape. Then he quickly covered it with the blanket. A couple of seconds later, he allowed a second puff of smoke to escape. And then a third. Finally, he completely doused the fire.

Three puffs of smoke meant that there was unusual activity, and the villagers were to be prepared to defend themselves in case of any hostility. This was definitely a faster way of communicating than running back to the village. The scout would also be able to send them regular updates if he concealed himself and observed the approachers.

Smoke signals were also used by the Chinese along the Great Wall. The Greeks, too, devised a system of smoke signals that could represent the letters of the alphabet, making it possible to send detailed and complex messages – possibly the world's first instance of texting!

28

I Spy with My Little Eye

Seeing far, seeing near, seeing clearly, seeing through sunglasses, seeing distant objects up close and seeing microscopic organisms appear huge... we humans have explored all avenues to stretch the limits of our natural vision.

3,000 years ago, in the Nimrud province of Assyria (modern-day Iraq)

The old man squinted at the slab of grey stone that he was carving. The delicate lines on the wings of the lion had looked so fine and elegant a few days ago but now they were blurred and hazy.

He called out to his assistant. 'Did anyone try anything "clever" on these carvings after I left?'

His assistant caught the tone of sarcasm in his master's voice and was surprised. 'No, sir, this exquisite carving is all your handiwork. Apart from admiring it, no one has done anything!'

'Why are all the fine lines gone, then?' the old man thundered.

The assistant shrank back, both frightened and confused. The lines looked perfectly fine to him.

The old man was the chief sculptor of the palace of the Assyrian king. He had more than 100 apprentices working under him, and he controlled them with a ferocious temper. He had set very high standards for the palace carvings; this was the only way he could ensure that everyone put in their best effort. After all, the carvings were done on the finest stone from the quarries, each one chosen after careful inspection for flaws and discolouration. Etched with the details of achievements of their great king and his forefathers, these carvings were made to last forever.

But what would not last forever was his eyesight.

He had suspected it but was not ready to accept it. Of late, even the king looked blurred and hazy to him, and he was sure no one had tampered with *His Majesty*! Perhaps his days as a sculptor were over.

Sighing, he moved on to the next item that a skilled group of apprentice sculptors was working on. They were executing the final details on the crown of the statue of the king. Everything looked hazy to the old man, but these were his best students, so he decided that the fault was with his own eyes. He squinted to see if it would get better. In the centre of the crown, they had made a shallow oval-shaped hollow. One sculptor picked up a piece of polished rock crystal and carefully began to set it in the hollow.

The old man blinked. For a split second, the carvings on the crown had stood out sharp and clear! What just happened?

It was the crystal!

Realizing this, just as the rock crystal was about to be set, the old man, to the utter astonishment of his students, plucked it away with an exclamation of delight. He bounded across the room, peering at every fine carving through the glass, shouting, 'I can see! I can see!'

He didn't have to give up sculpting just yet.

The Nimrud Lens

The oldest piece of 'lens' found so far was made by the Assyrians of Upper Mesopotamia. Estimated to have been created sometime between 750 BCE and 710 BCE, it is slightly oval, around 1.5 inches in diameter, ground and polished, and can magnify the image of an object up to three times its original size.

Nimrud lens displayed in the British Museum

Scholars are divided in opinion on what this lens might have been used for. Some say it was just a decorative piece of inlay, others say it was perhaps used as an eyeglass. Still others speculate that it might have been part of a telescope!

The reason for this last speculation is that the ancient Assyrians knew a great deal of advanced astronomy that they probably could not have picked up just by gazing at the sky with the naked eye. They have, for instance, described the planet Saturn as 'a god surrounded by a ring of serpents'. This does sound like a description of Saturn's rings!

What Would We Do without Glass?

A piece of rock crystal gave rise to a whole range of ideas, from magnifying glasses to lenses that curve, bifocals, telescopes, binoculars, cameras, microscopes, scanners and so many more devices. They all cleverly use glass to manipulate light into letting us see what our eyes fail to!

29

Learning to Fly

One foot on the ground, one foot in the air, she stood on the edge of the cliff, bracing against the strong wind that was whipping her hair around her face.

If I take one step forward, she thought, *will I fly or will I fall?*

Of course, you say, she will fall. And you would be right. But that can't stop her from dreaming, can it?

For centuries, humans have looked up at the sky and wondered if we would ever be able to swoop through the air and glide alongside birds, looking down below at the earth, as our trees and streets and buildings grow smaller and smaller, and we cut through the clouds and reach for the sun.

Let's start small, though. With a kite.

Second century BCE, China

General Han Xin's eyes narrowed as he surveyed the barren stretch of land between his military camp and the fortress he was preparing to invade. Like all good military strategists, he believed in planning well before attacking. This open territory before him offered no cover to his troops if the enemy began to shoot arrows while they advanced. So an open attack was out of the question.

He could bore a tunnel, though. That would work. Except he needed to know the exact distance between his camp and the fort. There seemed to be no way of measuring this distance without risking being seen and shot. Oh, how he wished he could fly! Wait... he had an idea.

He asked his people to construct a kite with the materials available in the camp. They used hollow bamboo sticks to make the frame of the kite and a sheer silk fabric for the sail. A spool of light, strong thread was attached to the kite.

Holding firmly on to the string, the general launched the kite in the direction of the fortress. He knew the length of the string released from the spool, so he was able to calculate the distance on the ground from his base camp to the fortress.

His engineers then dug a tunnel underneath and reached the fortress undetected.

Han Xin and other military strategists used the kite in various creative ways to gain advantage during war. They used kites to signal to their troops, sent noise makers up with the kites to distract the enemy, and lit up the sky with lanterns inside kites!

Lantern-filled kites were, strictly speaking, not kites at all but early forms of hot-air balloons. They were hollow rectangular lanterns, usually made with silk or paper, with an opening at the bottom where a small fire was suspended. Apart from creating a pretty picture in the sky, these lanterns were the beginnings of the idea that some sort of fuel could be used to power an object to fly. In this case, the little fire lit at the base of the lantern was the power source. The flame heated the air inside the lantern and caused its density to become lower than that of the surrounding air – and made the lantern fly!

It took us more than 1,000 years after this big idea to successfully build a hot-air balloon that could carry people. In the last part of the 18th century, the Montgolfier brothers sent people to a height of more than 400 metres and brought them safely back to earth.

But we didn't stop there. In a hot-air balloon, you didn't really feel like a bird, cutting and soaring and gliding through the air. Humans yearned for wings.

And so we made gliders.

One of the most successful models was Otto Lilienthal's, made during the last decade of the 19th century. It had two wings, and the flyer hung suspended between them, controlling the motion by shifting his or her weight. Following this stupendous success, Lilienthal made 16 different models, experimenting with aerodynamics and meticulously recording his observations. He would test his gliders by flying them himself. He made more than 2,000 flights in five years!

Before this, however, there were many experiments with flight. Some, like Leonardo da Vinci, had made detailed drawings on paper, while others had gone ahead

and built flying machines. A few of those machines took off, and many didn't. But they all contributed to that seminal moment in 1903 when the Wright brothers created history by piloting the first powered aircraft in Kitty Hawk, North Carolina. Orville Wright flew 20 feet above the ground for 12 seconds, covering 120 feet before making a safe, although bumpy, landing. The brothers made four more attempts to fly that day, with Wilbur making the longest flight – 59 seconds, covering a distance of 852 feet.

Did You Know

Amelia Earhart was the first woman to make a solo flight across the Atlantic in 1932.

30

Living in the Modern Age

This book, I had said in the beginning, is about the ideas that changed the course of history and defined humankind. You may have noticed that I have leaned more heavily towards the ancient world. To the ideas that provided the very first spark. We took that spark and built a fire that we could shape and mould and command. We hooked one great idea on to another, and then another, and we created technological marvels, pushing the boundaries of what previous generations thought was possible.

Ever since great civilizations grew from an agriculture-based economy, life was more or less moving on at a steady pace, until around 1760, when the Industrial Revolution took place. It moved the centre of production from farms and villages to factories and cities. But before I tell you what this was all about, let me tell you the story of power.

The first kind of power that humans harnessed was from their own muscles. So we built tools designed to make the best use of our strength, like the bow and arrow, spear, tools to dig and chip, ropes, pulleys, pedals, looms...

When we domesticated large animals, we harnessed their power. We used oxen to plough fields, horses to pull carriages, donkeys and llamas to carry loads and elephants to fell trees and move logs.

The big breakthrough came when we figured out a power source that was neither human nor animal in origin.

Sometime between 50 and 70 CE, Hero, a scientist who lived in Egypt (when it was ruled by the Romans), described a device that was powered by steam. It is not clear whether he invented this device or saw it somewhere, but it is the earliest mention of a steam-powered machine that we know of. He called it the aeolipile (pronounced ee-yo-li-pile, rhyming with smile).

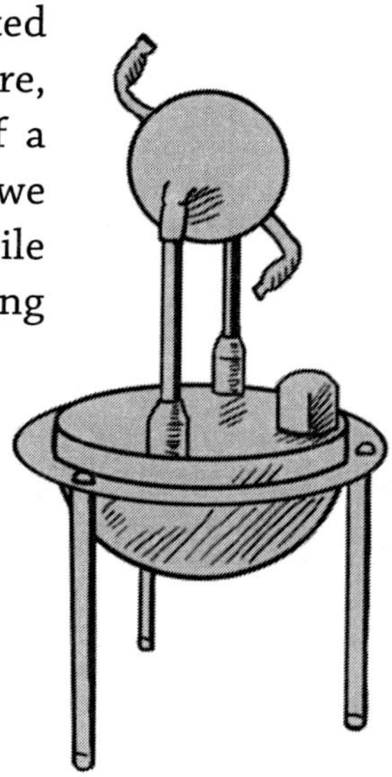

Hero described a vessel filled with water under which a fire is lit. The vessel is closed. Two tubes emerge from the lid and join a hollow sphere. This sphere has two nozzles, bent at right angles.

When the water boils, the steam enters the sphere through the tubes emerging from the lid. As steam escapes from one bent nozzle of the sphere, it creates a force that causes the sphere to revolve. Meanwhile, steam escaping from the other bent nozzle exerts an opposite force that causes it to revolve in the other direction. So you have a dancing figure, and for many years, it was considered just that, a contraption that provides entertainment.

Yet, it was the one thing that propelled the Industrial Revolution. The steam engine pushed the boundaries of human creation and ingenuity. It redefined ideas of manufacture, agriculture and transportation.

Just as 20,000 years ago, farming marked a point of no return for humanity, transforming us from nomads to settlers, the Industrial Revolution of the 18th century marked another important point in human history. It was not just about mechanization but also about the movement of large numbers of people from villages to cities. Because it was in the cities that factories were set up, creating jobs. Rural agrarian societies (mainly in Europe and America) transformed rapidly into urban centres of industrialization.

Having harnessed the power of steam, we soon stumbled upon coal, gas, oil and steel, ushering in the Second Industrial Revolution, this one powered by electricity.

Then, with one eye on the sun and another on the atom, we understood nuclear reactions and discovered a powerful new energy source. This, along with the emergence of electronics, bio and information technologies, defined all our processes anew – from the way we look at our environment to the way businesses are run, how we communicate, how we wage wars, how we make friends, how we perform surgeries, how we learn and how we work – and brought in the Digital Revolution.

Somewhere between the second and third revolutions, we discovered plastics. Cheap and easy to produce, they soon replaced wood, metal, stone and tusk in manufacture. It seemed like a miracle at first. We were no longer constrained by nature's fixed resources. We could make plastic at will, and we could make as much as we wanted. We started using and throwing, unmindful of what all this discarded plastic did. Now, we are starting to realize that plastics release toxins into the environment, harming life. What is more, every plastic that has ever been made continues to exist in some form on the earth. We are looking at huge mountains of plastic trash on land and islands in the oceans, and microplastics inside living creatures. It is clear that all ideas are not good ideas. We are an intelligent species, aren't we? Let's put our brains to good use and figure out a solution!

And assuming we do find a solution before we completely trash the planet, where do we go from there? What is left to discover? Are we at the brink of another revolution? In a bid to take over from human intelligence, we have started creating artificial intelligence. And in doing so, will we really discover ourselves?

What's *your* brilliant new idea?

Copyright Acknowledgements